# Tigers Along the Tigris

# Tigers Along the Tigris

The Leicestershire Regiment
in Mesopotamia During
the First World War

E. J. Thompson

*Tigers Along the Tigris: the Leicestershire Regiment in Mesopotamia During the First World War*
by E. J. Thompson

Originally published in 1919 under the title
*Beyond Baghdad With the Leicestershires*

Published by Leonaur Ltd

Text in this form copyright © 2007 Leonaur Ltd

ISBN: 978-1-84677-365-5 (hardcover)
ISBN: 978-1-84677-366-2 (softcover)

**http://www.leonaur.com**

Publisher's Note

The opinions expressed in this book are those of the author and are not necessarily those of the publisher.

# Contents

| | |
|---|---|
| Preface | 9 |
| Introduction | 13 |
| Beled | 19 |
| Harbe | 44 |
| The First Battle of Istabulat | 54 |
| The Battle for Samarra | 65 |
| Summer and Waiting | 96 |
| Huweslet; or, the Battle of Juber Island | 110 |
| Daur | 114 |
| Aujeh | 120 |
| Tekrit | 124 |
| Down to Busra | 133 |

To my brother
FRANK D. THOMPSON

Second-Lieutenant Civil Service Rifles
attached King's Royal Rifles
killed in action near Ypres
January 13th, 1917

*Our soldier youth thrice-loved, whose laughing face*
*In battle's front can danger meet with eyes*
*No fear could e'er surprise;*
*Nor stain of self in their gay love leave trace,*
*His nature like his name,*
*Frank, and his eager spirit pure as flame.*

Waltham Thickets

# Preface

The Mesopotamian War was a side-show, so distant from Europe that even the tragedy of Kut and the slaughter which failed to save our troops and prestige were felt chiefly in retrospect, when the majority of the men who suffered so vainly had gone into the silence of death or of captivity. When Maude's offensive carried our arms again into Kut, and beyond, to Baghdad, interest revived; but of the hard fighting which followed, which made Baghdad secure, nothing has been made known, or next to nothing. The men in Mesopotamia did not feel that this was unnatural. We felt, none more so, that it was the European War which mattered; indeed, our lot often seemed the harder by reason of its little apparent importance. Yet, after all, Baghdad was the first substantial victory which no subsequent reverse swept away; and it came when the need of victory, for very prestige's sake, was very great.

Mr. Candler has written, bitterly enough, of the way the Censorship impeded him in his work as official 'Eyewitness.' His was a thankless task; as he well knows, few of us, though we were all his friends, have not groused at his reports of our operations. No unit groused more on this head than my own division. We usually had a campaign and a bank of the Tigris to ourselves. 'Eye-witness' rightly chose to be with the other divisions across the river. Inevitably the 7th Meerut Division got the meagrest show in such meagre dispatches as the Censors allowed him to send home. The 2nd Leicestershires, an old and proud battalion, with the greatest of reputations on the field of action, remained unknown to the Press and public. Our other two British battalions, the 1st Seaforths and the 2nd Black Watch, could be referred to—even the Censors allowed this—as 'Highlanders'; and those who were interested knew that the reference lay between these two regiments and the Highland Light Infantry. But who was going to connect the rare reference to 'Midlanders' with the Leicestershires?

In May, 1917, the 7th Division tried to put together, for the Press, a connected account of their campaigning since Maude's offensive began. After various people, well qualified to do the work, had refused, it was devolved on me, on the simple grounds that a padre, as is well known, has only one day of work a week. The notion fell through. The authorities declined flatly to allow any reference to units by name, and no one took any more interest in a task so useless and soulless. But I had collected so much information from different units that I determined some day to try to put the story together. I have now selected two campaigns, those for railhead and for Tekrit, and made a straightforward narrative. From a multitude of such narratives the historian will build up his work hereafter.

An article by General Wauchope appeared in *Blackwood's*, 'The Battle that won Samarrah.' This article not only stressed the fact that the Black Watch were first in Baghdad and Samarra—an accident; they were the freshest unit on each occasion, while other units were exhausted from fighting just finished—but dismissed the second day of 'the battle that won Samarra' with one long paragraph, from which the reader could get no other meaning except the one that this day also was won by the same units as did the fighting of the 21st. This was a handling of fact which appealed neither to the Black Watch, whose achievements need no aid of embellishment from imagination, nor to the Leicestershires, who were made to appear spectators through the savage fighting of two days. If the reader turns to the chapter in this book entitled 'The Battle for Samarra,' he will learn what actually happened on April 22, 1917. The only other reference in print, that I know of, to the fighting for Samarra is the chapter in Mr. Candler's book. This, he tells us, was largely taken over by him from a journalist who visited our battlefields during the lull of summer. He showed the account to officers of my division, myself among them, and they added a few notes. But the chapter remained bare and comparatively uninteresting beside the accounts of actions which Mr. Candler had witnessed.

For this book, then, my materials have been: First, my own experience of events *quorum ego pars minima*. Next, my own note-books, carefully kept over a long period in Mesopotamia and Palestine, a period from which these two campaigns of Samarra and Tekrit have been selected. Thirdly, I saw regimental war-diaries and talked with brigade and regimental officers. Most of all, from the Leicestershires I gained information. It is rarely any use to question men about an action; even if they speak freely, they say little which is of value on the printed page. One may live with a regimental mess for months, running into years, as I did with the Leicestershires' subalterns, and hear little that is illuminating, till some electric spark may start a fire of living reminiscence. But from many of my comrades, at one time and another, I have picked up a fact. I am especially indebted to Captain J.O.C. Hasted, D.S.O., for permission to use his lecture on the Samarra battle. I could have used this lecture still more with great gain; but I did not wish to impair its interest in itself, as it should be published. From Captain F.J. Diggins, M.C., I gained a first-hand account of the capture of the Turkish guns. And Major Kenneth Mason, M.C., helped me with information in the Tekrit fighting. My brother, Lieutenant A.R. Thompson, drew the maps.

In conclusion, though the Mesopotamian War was of minor importance beside the fighting in Western Europe, for the chronicler it has its own advantages. If our fighting was on a smaller scale, we saw it more clearly. The 7th Division, as I have said, usually had a campaign, with its battles, to themselves. We were not a fractional part of an eruption along many hundreds of miles; we were our own little volcano. And it was the opinion of many of us that on no front was there such comradeship; yet many had come from France, and two divisions afterwards saw service on the Palestine front. Nor can any front have had so many grim jokes as those with which we kept ourselves sane through the long-drawn failure before Kut and the dragging months which followed.

# Introduction

On November 6, 1914, Brigadier-General Delamaine captured Fao forts, and the Mesopotamian War began in the smallest possible way, the proverbial 'corporal's guard' breaking into an empire.

The next twelve months saw a great deal of fighting, unorthodox in every way, carried through in appalling weathers and with the most inadequate forces.

In the three days' battle at Shaiba, in April, defeat was hardly escaped.

In April and May General Gorringe conducted the Ahwaz operations, near the Persian border, with varying success, and threatened Amara, on the Tigris, midway between Busra and Baghdad.

In May Townshend began his advance up-country. By June 3 he had taken Q'urna, where Tigris and Euphrates mingle; presently his miscellaneous marine and a handful of men took Amara, in what was known as 'Townshend's Regatta.' Seventeen guns and nearly two thousand prisoners were taken at Amara.

In the heats of July, incredible as it sounds, Gorringe was fighting on the Euphrates, by Nasiriyeh, taking twenty-one guns and over a thousand prisoners.

On September 28 Townshend won his last victory at Kut-el-Amara, taking fourteen guns and eleven hundred prisoners. Every one knows what followed: how Ctesiphon was fought in November, with four thousand five hundred and sixty-seven casualties, and how his force raced back to Kut. On December 7 Kut was invested by the Turks. Townshend's stand here saved the lower country to us.

Relief forces disembarked at Ali Gharbi, between Amara and Kut, and some of the bitterest fighting the world has seen began. Sheikh Saad (January 6 to 8) was a costly victory. A gleam of hope came with the Russian offensive in Northern Asia Minor. On January 13, at the Wadi, six miles beyond Sheikh Saad and less than thirty miles from Kut, the Turks held us up, but slipped away in the night.

All advancing was over flat ground devoid of even scrub-cover, through a region the most desolate in the world. Above Amara there is a place called 'Lone-Tree Village,' which has a small tree ten feet high. Except for a handful of draggled palms at Sheikh Saad, this tree is the only one till Kut is reached, on a river frontage of sixty miles.

On January 20 the British suffered a heavy repulse at Umm-el-Hanna, five miles beyond the Wadi. For nearly seven weeks our troops sat down in the swamps, and died of disease. The rains were abnormal.

On March 8 a long flank march up the right bank of the Tigris took the enemy by surprise, and reached Dujaileh, less than ten miles from Kut. Time was wasted in an orthodox but unnecessary bombardment. The Turks swarmed back into the redoubt, and we were bloodily thrust back, and returned to our lines before Hanna, with heavy losses in men and transport. After that very few cherished any hope of saving Kut.

April was a month of terrible fighting, frontal attacks on

a very brave and exultant enemy. The 13th Division, from Gallipoli, took the Hanna trenches, which were practically deserted, on April 5. The day went well for us. In the afternoon Abu Roman lines on the right bank, and in the evening those of Felahiyeh on the left bank, were carried by storm. But next day the first of the five battles of Sannaiyat was fought. We were repulsed.

The Turk's procedure was easy. He shot us down as we advanced over flat country. We dug ourselves in four hundred yards away (say). Then we sapped up to within storming distance, and attacked again, to find that the lines were thinly held, with a machine-gun or two, but that another position awaited us beyond, at the end of a long level sweep of desert.

On April 9 came the second battle of Sannaiyat. The time has not come to speak frankly of this day; but our men lay in heaps. So from the 16th to the 18th we tried frontal attacks on the other bank, the right again. This was the battle of Beit Aiessa. We did so well that the enemy had to counter-attack, which he did in the most determined manner, forcing us back. It cost him at least three thousand dead; but by this day's work he made sure of Kut and its garrison. Our one hope now was in the Russians. But their offensive halted; and we fought, on the 22nd, the third of the Sannaiyat battles. On the 29th, after a siege of one hundred and forty-three days, Kut surrendered, and with it the biggest British force ever taken by any enemy.

A summer inexpressibly harassing and depressed followed; but towards the end of 1916 affairs were reorganized, and at last a general was found. On the night of December 13 we crossed the Shat-el-Hai, and Maude's attack on Kut began. Ten weeks of fighting, very little interrupted by the weather, followed. It was stern work, hand-to-hand and trench-to-trench, as in France. By the end of the third week in February Kut was doomed. The Turk had made the mistake of leaving small, unsupported groups of men in angles and corners of the Tigris. Maude destroyed these, and between the 22nd and the 25th launched his final attacks simultaneously on both banks. A badly managed attack on Sannaiyat had failed on the 17th; but now, on the 22nd, the lines were stormed. Fighting continued here, and the river was crossed and bridged behind the Turks, above Kut, at Shumran. The Sannaiyat garrison fled precipitately, and the 7th Indian Division occupied successively the Nakhailat and Suwada lines with no opposition worth mentioning. Kut fell automatically, the monitors steaming in and taking possession. The infantry had no time to bother about it. Kut had become a symbol only.

So the infantry swung by Kut and on to Baghdad. The cavalry and gunboats hunted the enemy northward, till he made a stand on the Diyaleh, a large stream entering the Tigris a few miles below Baghdad. Very heavy fighting and losses had come to the 13th Division, and the 7th Division would be the first to acknowledge that the honour of first entering Baghdad, for whatever it was worth, should have fallen to them. But, in spite of desperate attempts to cross, they were held on the Diyaleh. The 7th Division therefore bridged the river lower down, and after two days of battle in a sandstorm, blind with thirst—for the men had one water-bottle only for the two days—captured Baghdad railway-station, and threw pickets across the river into Baghdad town. This was on March 11. The 13th and 14th Divisions then crossed the Diyaleh, and were in Baghdad almost as soon as any one from the 7th Division. The 7th and 3rd Indian Divisions passed by Baghdad on opposite sides, as they had passed by Kut, and engaged the enemy's rearguards at Mushaidiyeh and in the Jebel Hamrin. They then concentrated again towards Baghdad.

This book deals first with the April campaign as it affected the right bank of the Tigris. Between Baghdad and Samarra was a stretch of eighty miles of railroad, the only completed portion, south of Mosul, of the Berlin-Baghdad Railway. If we could capture this the Turk would have to supply his troops from Mosul by the treacherous and shallow Tigris. The Samarra fighting, these railhead battles, was the last organized campaign which the Turk fought. Our First Corps, consisting of two Indian divisions, the 3rd and the 7th, operated against railhead; while the Third Corps, consisting of the 13th Division, the only all-British division in Mesopotamia, and the 14th Indian Division, fought their way up the left bank.

After Samarra fell the Turk could do nothing but collect small bodies of troops, which we attacked in detail, usually with success, and throughout 1918, after Tekrit, always attacked with complete success (as we did at Ramadie in September, 1917, destroying the whole force). Ramadie, on the Euphrates, and Tekrit, on the Tigris, were the first of the campaigns of this last phase of the Mesopotamian War, campaigns that were glorified raids. At the time of Tekrit, General Allenby settled for the Turk, once for all, the choice between Palestine and Mesopotamia.

Our Tekrit campaign was a sympathetic attack, concurrent with Allenby's great Gaza offensive. This campaign is the theme of the second portion of this book.

# Chapter 1
# Beled

*Red of gladiolus glimmering through the wheat—*
*Red flower of Valour springing at our feet!*
*Dark-flowered hyacinth mingling with the red—*
*Dark flower of Patience on the way we tread!*
*Scarlet of poppy waving o'er the grass—*
*Honour's bright flags along the road we pass!*
*Thorns that torment, and grassy spikes that fret,*
*Thistles that all the fiery way beset!*
*These shall be theirs, when Duty's day is sped;*
*They shall lie down, the living and the dead.*

### The Way to Beled

Baghdad fell on March 11, 1917. The soldier's joy was deepened by the belief that here his warfare was accomplished, his marching finished. Even when we went by the city, and fought battles on either bank, the 7th Indian Division at Mushaidiyeh (March 14) and the 3rd Indian, most disastrously, in the foothills of the Jebel Hamrin (March 25), this comfort was not destroyed. These two hard actions were but the sweeping away of ants' nests from before a house; our position now secured, we should fall back, and rest in Baghdad. The Turk might try to turn us out; but that was a very different affair, and it would be months before he could even dream of an offensive.

So in April the 7th Division had withdrawn to Baghdad, all except the 28th Brigade, who were at Babi, a dozen miles up-stream. At Babi it was not yet desert—there was grass and wheat; but the garden-belt and trees had finished.

On the 3rd came official news that Tennant, of the R.F.C., had landed among the Cossacks, and been tumultuously welcomed; presently we heard that the Russians and ourselves had joined hands. This was towards the Persian border, on the left bank of the Tigris, where the 13th and 14th Divisions were operating. That force and ours, the 7th, were now to advance together on Samarra; a new campaign was beginning, in which we took the right bank.

A Mobile Column was formed, under Brigadier-General Davies, as the spearhead of the 7th Division's thrust. It consisted of the 28th Infantry Brigade (2nd Leicestershires, 51st and 53rd Sikhs, 56th Rifles, and 136th Machine-Gun Company), the 9th Brigade, R.F.A. (less one battery), one section of the 524th Battery, R.F.A., a Light-Armoured Motor-Battery, the 32nd Lancers (less two squadrons), and a half-company of Sappers and Miners; an ammunition column and ambulances.

Fritz—the enemy's airman—inspected us before we started. Then the Leicestershires, by twelve and eight miles, marched in two days to a point opposite Sindiyeh, on the Tigris. The Indian battalions cut across country to Sumaikchah, which lies inland.

That day and night by Sindiyeh! *'Infandum jubes renovare dolorem.'* The day was one of burning discomfort, spent in cracks and *nullas*, under blanket bivouacs. We had tramped, from dawn, through eight miles of 'chivvy-dusters,' and our camp was now among them. These are a grass which crams the clothes and feet with maddening needles; once in they seemed there 'for duration.' The soldier out East knows them for his worst foe on a march. Lest we should be obsessed with these, we were infested with sandflies and mosquitoes. But large black ants were the principal line in vermin. At dinner they swarmed over us. Man after man dropped his plate and leapt into a dervish-dance, frenziedly slapping his nose and ears. We tried to eat standing; even so, we were festooned. Little Westlake, the 'Cherub,' abandoned all hope of nourishment, and crept wretchedly into a clothes-pile. There was no sleep that night.

The river ran beneath lofty bluffs; on the left bank was a far-stretching view of low, rich country, with palms and canals. Fritz visited us, and a monitor favoured us with some comically bad shooting. And after sundown came a moon, benignant, calm, in a cloudless heaven, looking down on men miserable with small vexations, which haply saved them from facing too much the deeper griefs which accompanied them.

Next morning, Good Friday, we joined the rest of the column at Sumaikchah. The Cherub with his scouts went ahead to find a road. All the field was jumping with grasshoppers, on which storks were feeding. Scattered bushes looked in the mirage like enemy patrols. We were escorted by Fritz, whose kindly interest in our movements never flagged. We started late, at 6.50 a.m., and without breakfast, the distance being under-estimated. A zigzagging course made the journey into over ten miles, in dreadful heat; we were marching till past noon. When Sumaikchah came in sight, men fell out, exhausted, in bunches and groups.

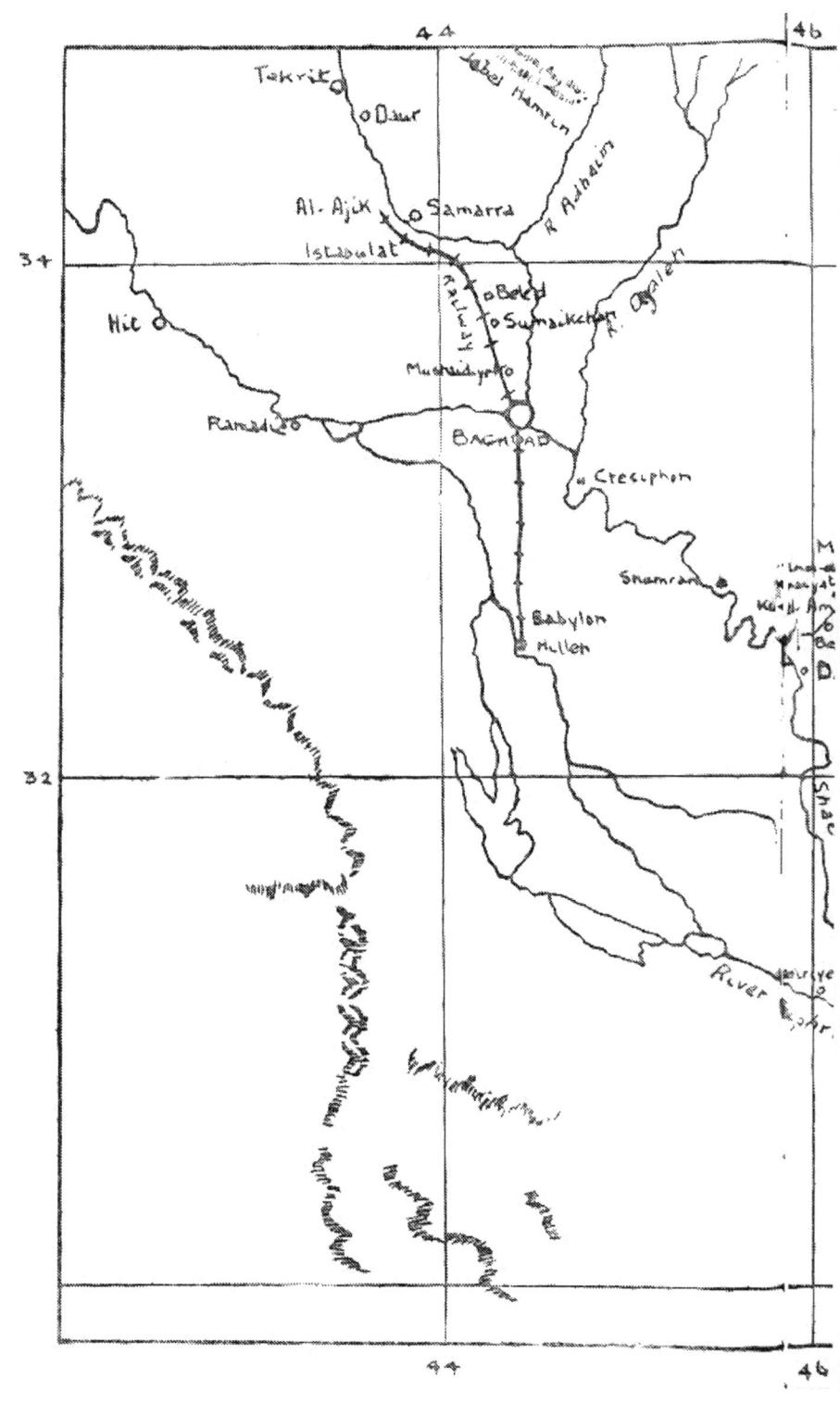

Though we were unmolested, the countryside was full of eyes. Shortly afterwards an artillery officer, bringing up remounts, sent a Scots sergeant ahead to Sumaikchah, with a strong escort, to bring back rations. The party was fired on by Buddus. The sergeant's report attained some fame; deservedly, so I give it here:

'We were fired on, sirrr.'

'Did you fire back?'

'No, sirrr. I thocht it would have enrrraged them. But I'd have ye know, sirrr, that it's hairrrdly safe to be aboot.'

We came, says Xenophon, to 'a large and thickly populated city named Sittake.' His troops encamped 'near a large and beautiful park, which was thick with all sorts of trees, at a distance of fifteen stades from the river.'[1] This description still holds true of Sumaikchah. The ancient irrigation channels are dry, and the town has shrunken; but it remains a large garden-village. Here were melons and oranges, fowls and turkeys, exorbitantly priced, of course; possibly Xenophon's troops got their goods more cheaply in the year 399 B.C.

Sumaikchah is an oasis with eighty wells. The water was full of salts. It was bad as water; it was execrable as tea. Many of the wells on the Baghdad-Samarra Railway have these natural salts. Every one who left Sumaikchah next morning was suffering from diarrhoea. Here again one remembers the *Anabasis* and the troublesome experience which the notes I read at school ascribed to poisonous honey gathered from the flowers of *rhododendron ponticum*.

Our brief stay here was unlike anything we had known, except in our racing glimpse of the flowery approaches to

---

[1] *Anabasis*, Book ii., H.G. Dakyns' translation. The identification of Sumaikchah and Sittake is due to Major Kenneth Mason, R.E., M.C.

Kut. The village had palms and rose bushes. A coarse hyacinth, found already at Mushaidiyeh, now seeding, grew along the railway and in the wheat. We camped amid green corn; round us were storksbills, very many, and a white *orchis*, slight and easily hidden, the same *orchis* that I found afterwards in Palestine and in the Hollow Vale of Syria. A small poppy and a bright thistle set their flares of crimson and gold in the green; sowthistle and myosote freaked it with blue; a tall gladiolus, also to be found later by the Aujeh and on Carmel, made pink clusters. Thus did flowers overlay the fretting spikes of our road, and adorn and hide 'the coming bulk of Death.'

Through Saturday we rested. Fritz came, of course; and there was a little harmless sniping.

The knowledge filtered in that fighting was again at hand. It was accepted without comment, with the soldier's well-known fatalism, the child of faith and despair. 'Every man thinks,' said one to me, 'I don't care who he is. But we believe it's all right till our number's up. Take M——, for instance. When he was left out at Sannaiyat we all envied him; we thought we were for it. But we went through Sannaiyat; and M—— was the first of us to be killed at Mushaidiyeh, his very first action, where we had hardly any casualties.'

In the evening the rest of the division came up to take our place. Sunday, by old prescription, was the 7th Division's battle-day; next Sunday being Easter, it was not to be supposed that so fair an occasion would be passed over. Accordingly, when I put in my services, I was told that the brigade would march before dawn, and that some scrapping was anticipated. The Turks were holding Beled Station, half a dozen miles away in a straight line. Their main force was at Harbe, four miles farther. The maps were no use, and distances had to be guessed. 'The force against us,' observed the Brigade-Major, 'is somewhere between a hundred Turks and two guns, and four thousand Turks and thirty-two guns.' 'And if it's the four thousand and thirty-two guns?' 'Then we shall sit tight, and scream for help,' he answered delightedly.

## THE ACTION FOR BELED

Davies's Column were away before breakfast. In the dim light we moved through wet fields of some kind of globe-seeded plant, abundantly variegated with gladiolus and hyacinth. Every one was suffering from our course of Sumaikchah waters, and progress was slow. Splashing through the marshes, we came to undulating upland, long, steady slopes, pebble-strewn and with pockets of grass and poppies. The morning winds made these uplands exceedingly beautiful. Colonel Knatchbull said, the week he died, that what he most remembered from Beled were the flowers through which we marched to battle. As we approached them, the ruffling wind laid its hand on the grasses, and they became emerald waves, a green spray of blades tossing and flashing in the full sunlight. As we passed, the same wind bowed them before it, and they were a shining, silken cloth. The poppies were a larger sort than those in the wheat fields, and of a very glorious crimson. In among the grasses was yellow coltsfoot; among the pebbles were sowthistle, mignonette, pink bindweed, and great patches of storksbill. Many noted the beauty of these flowers, a scene so un-Mesopotamian in its brightness. We were tasting of the joy and life of springtide in happier latitudes, a wine long praetermitted to our lips; and among us were those who would not drink of this wine again till they drank it new in their Father's Kingdom. After Beled we saw no more flowers.

With the first line was my friend Private W——. As we pushed forward he looked up, as his custom was, for a 'message.' Perchance, with so many fears and hopes stirring, there was some buzzing along the heavenly wires; but the only word he could get was this one, 'Because.' He puzzled upon it, till the whole flashed on his brain—*'Because Thy loving kindness is better than life, my lips shall praise Thee.'* Thenceforward he went his ways content; neither can any man have gathered greater pleasure from the beauty of the morning and those unwonted flowers than this Plymouth Brother, a gardener by profession, and, as I found in later days, amid the rich deep meadows of the Holy Land, a passionate lover of all wild plants.

The left flank was guarded by one section of machine-gunners and one section of the 32nd Lancers. Next to them moved the Leicestershires. Some time after 8 a.m. rifle-fire on our left told us that the Cherub's scouts were in touch with enemy patrols. About 9.30 the first shell came, our advanced guard being some five thousand yards from Beled Station.

There were frequent halts, while our few cavalry reconnoitred. Then we passed into a deep broad *nulla* between two ancient earth-walls. All this terrain had been a network of canals and cultivation. Shrapnel was bursting in our front. We filed out, at the left, on to a plain. Half a mile ahead was the nearer curve of a hilly ground. The main range ran in a Carpathian-like sweep across our front, from west to east; turned, and went across our front again. Beyond this was Beled Station, lying at the point of a wide fork of hills, the left prong a good mile away, but the right bending almost up to it. From the forking to the station was a broken plain of two thousand yards. This plain had to be overcome, with such assistance as the hills gave. The hills were pretty uniform in height, and nowhere above thirty feet. The railway cut directly through the main range, giving the enemy a field of fire for his machine-guns. The range, with its double fold across our front, gave the artillery cover, and enabled us to conceal the smallness of our force; and on both sides of the station it broke into a wilderness of little knobs and hollows, by which we might creep up.

The shrapnel was uncomfortably close as we crossed to the first sweep of hilly ground. But it was bursting high, and no casualties occurred. We halted behind the hills, and the artillery left their wagons, taking their guns into position where the range curved north-westerly. Here two four-gun batteries put up a slow and not heavy bombardment on the station. We waited and watched the shrapnel bursting five hundred yards to our right. About noon the Leicestershires were ordered to support the 53rd and 51st Sikhs in an attack on the station. (The 56th Rifles were in reserve throughout the action.) D Company was to move on the left of the railway as a flank-guard, and went forward under Captain Creagh.

I must now speak of Second-Lieutenant Fowke, our tallest subaltern. In place of the orthodox shade of khaki he wore a reddish-brown shooting-jacket, which shimmered like bright silk if there was any sun. Nevertheless he was the only Leicestershire subaltern who went through all our battles unwounded. Of his cheerfulness and courage, his wit, and the love with which his colleagues and his men regarded him, the reader will learn. Fowke was detached with his platoon to act on our extreme left in co-operation with our handful of Indian cavalry. The operation was an undesirable one, to advance into a maze of tiny hills, held by an enemy of unknown strength; and as Fowke moved off I remembered the Sieur de Joinville's *Memoirs* and a passage mentioned between us the previous day. So, as I wished him good luck, I said, 'Be of good cheer, seneschal, for we shall yet talk over this day in the ladies' bowers.' Once upon a time Fowke had read for Holy Orders, a fact which contributed not a little to the astonishment and delight with which he was regarded. He smiled gravely in answer to me, and moved on. But after the scrap he told me that he wished just then that he had continued in his first vocation and become a padre.

Behind D Company moved Charles Copeman, O.C. bombers, and a section of machine-gunners under Lieutenant Service. The rest of the machine-gunners followed up along the railway.

We who remained crossed the ridge and advanced in artillery formation up the right side of the railway. The Sikhs slipped away into the hills to our right.

Readers of *Quentin Durward* will remember the two hangmen of Louis XI, the one tall, lean, and solemn; the other short, fat, and jolly. Wilson, the Leicestershires' doctor, had two most excellent assistants who occupied much the same positions. But Sergeant Whitehead, who was short, went his sombre way with a gravity that never weakened into a smile; while Dobson, an ex-miner, aged forty-seven, who had deceived the recruiting people most shamelessly and enlisted as under thirty, took life jovially and generally humorously. He was never without his pipe. He enjoyed a large medical practice in the regiment, unofficial and unpaid, and he held strong opinions, observing frequently that he 'didn't hold with' a thing. I remember well the annoyance of Wilson's successor on hearing that Dobson 'didn't hold with' inoculation, which just then was occupying most of the medical officer's time. Another thing that Dobson 'didn't hold with' was the modern notion that some diseases were infectious. Because of his years and medical knowledge, this kindly, never-wearied old hero was always known by the regiment as 'Mester Dobson.' I shall follow their example, and so call him henceforth.

I also was of Wilson's entourage, and went with him accordingly. Before we crossed the first ridge we picked up a man prostrate with heat-stroke; we left him under a culvert, in charge of John, Wilson's Indian orderly.

Meanwhile D Company found the hills on our left strongly held. Every slope was sown with shallow trenches, earth-scars which held six or seven Turks, and snipers caused us casualties. Lieutenant-Colonel Knatchbull, learning this, on his own initiative swung round B and C Companies across the railway to support D. Wilson now came upon his first casualty, a signaller hit in the spine. We bandaged him, and left him in a shallow *nulla*, sheltered from the bullets flying over. He died next day.

B and C Companies, crossing the railway, pushed up a long narrow *nulla* to the hills where D were engaged. Service's machine-guns put up a covering fire.

The attack had now developed along two distinct lines, and on the railway itself we had no troops. The enemy presently put down a barrage of shrapnel all the right length of the line, where he had seen our men cross, of which barrage every shell during two hours was wasted. As Wilson dropped down the embankment on our left side of the railway, we found machine-gunners sheltering in a quarry, awaiting orders.

'It's unhealthy over there,' said their O.C., Lieutenant Sanderson. 'The Turks have a machine-gun on it.'

However, there was a lull as we crossed to the *nulla*, and only a very few bullets went by. In the *nulla* Wilson set up his aid-post, sticking a second flag above the railway, for the solitary company that was supporting the Sikhs' attack. Wounded began to come in, the first cases being not bad ones.

'Give you five rupees for that wound, sergeant,' said Mester Dobson.

'You can't have it for seventy-five,' said Sergeant Hayes, as he limped off in search of the ambulances, smiling happily.

Perhaps nothing will stir the unborn generations to greater pity than this knowledge, that for youth in our generation wounds and bodily hurt were a luxury.

But cases soon came in of men badly hit, in much pain. With them was borne a dead man, Sergeant Lawrence, D.C.M., a quiet and much-liked man. My Plymouth Brother friend came also, and sat aside, saying he could wait, as a stretcher-case was following him. As the doctor saw to that broken body, my friend rested his wounded leg, and we had some talk. The long marches, the nights of little sleep, and the unsheltered days of heat and toil and wearied waiting for evening had tired him out.

'I want rest,' he said, 'and I think the Lord knows it, and has sent rest along.' All our men were brave and cheerful, but no more cheerful hero limped off through the bullets than my calm and gentle friend.

Wilson went out for a few minutes to see a man in the second line, hit in the groin. When he returned we had some cruelly broken cases in, and that *nulla* saw a deal of pain, and grew stale with the smell of blood. A fair number of bullets flew over, and there was the occasional swish of a machine-gun. Mules were killed far back in the second line, and men hit. But the *nulla* was safe. The misguided Turk shelled and machine-gunned the empty space beyond the railway.

Colonel Knatchbull came in and assured Wilson that the *nulla* was the best and most central place for the aid-post. He searched the front with his glasses. Then he said, 'Marner's dead.'

The Leicestershires' attack was held up in the hills. They asked for support, but none was available. They were told to advance as far as they could, and then hold their line till help could come. The hills were thick with excellent positions. Every fold and dip was utilized by a scattered and numerous foe, to whom the ragged ground was like a cloak of invisibility. No artillery help could be given. We could only seize the ground's advantage and make it serve as help to the attack as well as to the defence. It was here that Marner fell. C Company was sheltering in an ancient canal. Seeing a man fall, Captain Hasted called out, 'Keep your heads down.' Almost at that moment Marner looked over, having spotted a sniper who was vexing us, and fell dead at Grant-Anderson's feet. Though in falling he brushed against Hasted, the latter could not pause to see who it was; nor did he know till he cried out, a minute later, that Marner was to move round the flank of the position immediately before them. Some two hundred yards farther on Second-Lieutenant Otter was struck by a bullet which went through both left arm and body, a bad but not fatal wound. But a gracious thought came to the Turkish gunners. Seeing us without artillery support from our own guns, they put two rounds of shrapnel over, the only shells on these ridges during the fight. These burst directly on the Turkish snipers, who did not wait for the hint to be repeated, but went. The Leicestershires topped the last ridge, and were on the plain before the station. Fowke and Service remained to guard the left flank, while Hasted went forward with the bayonet to clear the hills to the left. Fowke, watching benevolently the evolutions of certain horsemen on his left, received a message from our cavalry, 'Those are Arabs on your left, and are hostile to you.'

And now it would have meant a bloody advance for A and B Companies against those trenches in the open. But the Turks, held by the Leicestershires' strong steady attack, had given insufficient attention to the movement threatening their left. The two Sikh regiments, though checked and held from time to time by rifle and machine-gun fire, used the broken ground with extraordinary skill. Their experience on the Afghan frontier had trained them for just such work as this. Rising ground was used as positions for covering fire, and every knoll and hummock became a shoulder to lift the force along. Their supporting battery had located the enemy's gun-positions, and kept down his fire. One gun-team bolted, and the crew were seen getting the gun away by hand and losing in the effort. The Sikhs rushed a low hill, which had long checked them, and its garrison of one officer and twenty-five men surrendered. This attack was led by the well-known 'Boomer' Barrett, colonel of the 51st. He slapped the nearest prisoner on the back and bellowed *'Shabash.'*[2] The enemy's resistance crumbled rapidly. A breach had been made in his defence, and the Sikhs poured through. They made two thousand yards, and did a swift left-turn. The enemy on their right slipped off, but the Turks in the trenches covering the station had left things too late. The 51st drove the foe before them to the north of the station, and the 53rd

---

[2] 'Well done' (Hindustani).

rushed the station itself, capturing eight officers and a hundred and thirty-five men, with two machine-guns. This was about 3 p.m.

Wilson now left his aid-post, and we came up the line. All the way the Turk was shelling the railway, but, by that fortunate defect of observation conspicuous throughout, shelling our right exclusively, for not a shell came on the left. We passed the enemy's trenches and rifle-pits, which scarred some six or seven hundred yards of space before the station; there were rifles leaning against the walls, with bayonets fixed.

The station had excellent water, a great attraction after the filthy wells of Sumaikchah. No one heeded that the Turk was dropping shells two thousand yards our side of the station. 'He always does that. It's a sort of rearguard business. It's the ammunition he can't get away. He'll be moving his guns quickly enough when we get ours on to them.' But, as the official report afterwards observed, with just annoyance at the enemy's refusal to recognize that the action was finished:

> During the whole of the afternoon and till dusk the enemy continued to shell the captured position with surprising intensity, considering what had been heard of his shortage in gun-ammunition.

What happened, in fuller detail, was this.

Beled Station was like the gate of Heaven. With the exception of the Leicestershires, still in the field, all the great and good were gathered there. The first I saw was that genial philosopher, Captain Newitt, of the 53rd Sikhs, sitting imperturbable on a fallen wall and smoking the pipe without which he has never been seen. Not Marius amid Carthage ruins was more careless of the desolation around him. With him was Culverwell, adjutant of the same battalion. They hailed me with joyous affection, and we drank the waters and swapped the news.

General Davies came up and asked, 'Have the Leicesters taken any prisoners?'

I told him 'No.'

He seemed disappointed; then added, 'We've taken over two hundred prisoners, including nine officers and three machine-guns. What were your casualties?'

'About twenty, sir,' I said.

'The 53rd have had thirteen men wounded,' said the Brigade-Major. 'Fifty will cover the casualties for the whole brigade. It's been a most successful action.'

Marner's loss was greatly felt. 'I hear you've lost a good officer,' said the Brigadier; and the Brigade-Major added:

'He was the brigade's great stand-by for maps and drawings. I don't know how we can replace him.'

Then for a moment we fell to jape and jesting; foolishly, for the Gods are always listening, and the Desert-Gods have long ears.

'You're last from school,' said Brigade-Major McLeod. 'You know Napier's message—"*Peccavi*, I have Sind." Give me a wire for Corps, "I have B-led."'

'*Sanguinevi*,' I said, 'if such a verb exists. Let's call it very late Latin.'

As we spoke, the enemy shortened his range; a shell skimmed the roof, and burst at the embankment bottom, directly under two Sikhs who were cooking. It hurled one man into the air and the other to one side. A great dust went up. Before most people realized what had happened, Wilson and Stones were carrying the men up the bank. This was an extremely brave deed, for a second shell was certain, and, as a matter of fact, a second and a third came just as they had reached our wall. Stones, like many medical officers, was a missionary; he had come from West Africa. He had one of the noblest faces I ever saw; a very gentle and courteous man, fearless and with eager eyes. He served with the 56th Rifles.

One of the stricken men was a mass of bleeding ribbons, the top of his head blown off. A cloth was drawn over his face; he was dead. The other had his left leg torn off below the knee, his right heel blown away, and wounds in his head and stomach. He died that evening. Now he lay with scarcely a moan, while Sikhs gathered round and gave such consolation as was possible, an austere, brave group.

The Turkish gunners now concentrated on the station and its approaches. Our cavalry rode through the Leicestershires' lines as those warriors moved up to an advanced line of defence. They brought a wounded prisoner. The enemy instantly shrapnelled them, and they scattered, the prisoner, for all his broken leg, keeping his seat excellently and riding surprisingly fast. Luck had been with the battalion this day, and it now remained with them. Many had rifles hit. Fowke, who was a magnet for bullets, had his right shoulder's star flattened. But there were no casualties. The enemy, growing vindictive, chased small bodies of even three or four with shrapnel. He continued to pelt the station, throwing at least two hundred rounds on it in two hours. Mules and horses were hit, and many men. Isolated men, holding horses in the open, had a bad time. Several shells landed on the roof, and had there been against us the huge guns of other fronts the station would have gone up in dust. When I saw it again, a month later, I realized what a rough house that tiny spot had experienced. Unexploded shells were still in the walls, and on the inner wall of the side that had sheltered me I counted over twenty direct hits. Fortunately the 5.9's were not in action this day, and every station on the Baghdad-Samarra line has been built as a fortress, massively. By incredible luck no shell came through the doorless openings and rooms behind us; they struck the inner wall and roof. But the water-station behind us gave very poor shelter to the men there. Shells burst on the railway, and sent a sheet of smoke and rubble before them. Two of our guns came up to the hills that had covered the Sikhs' advance, but fired very few shells, failing to find a target. The enemy saw their flashes, and fired back without effect. Then Fritz came and hovered above our huddled crowd with low, deliberate circles. We took it for granted he would bomb us, or, at kindest, spot for his guns. But he just hung over us, and then went to look for our batteries.

Before this McLeod offered me a cup of tea. We drank it in a tin shed a few yards south of the station. I wanted the tea horribly, but felt it was 'hairrdly safe to be aboot.'

This feeling was shared, for when the staff-captain and signalling-officer joined us, the latter asked, 'Isn't this spot a bit unhealthy, sir?'

'Oh, no,' said McLeod. 'It's quite safe from splinters, and it's no use bothering about a direct hit.'

As I had seen high explosive burst pretty well all round, and both windows were smashed of every inch of glass, I could not quite share this confidence that the hut was splinter-proof. But I required that tea. It was very good tea. Had it been shaving water, it would have gone cold at once. But being tea which I wished to drink quickly, it remained at boiling-point and declined to be mollified with milk. However, no more H.E.[3] came our way, only shrapnel.

McLeod said we had had at least two thousand Turks against us and at least twelve guns. During the action the

---

[3] High explosive.

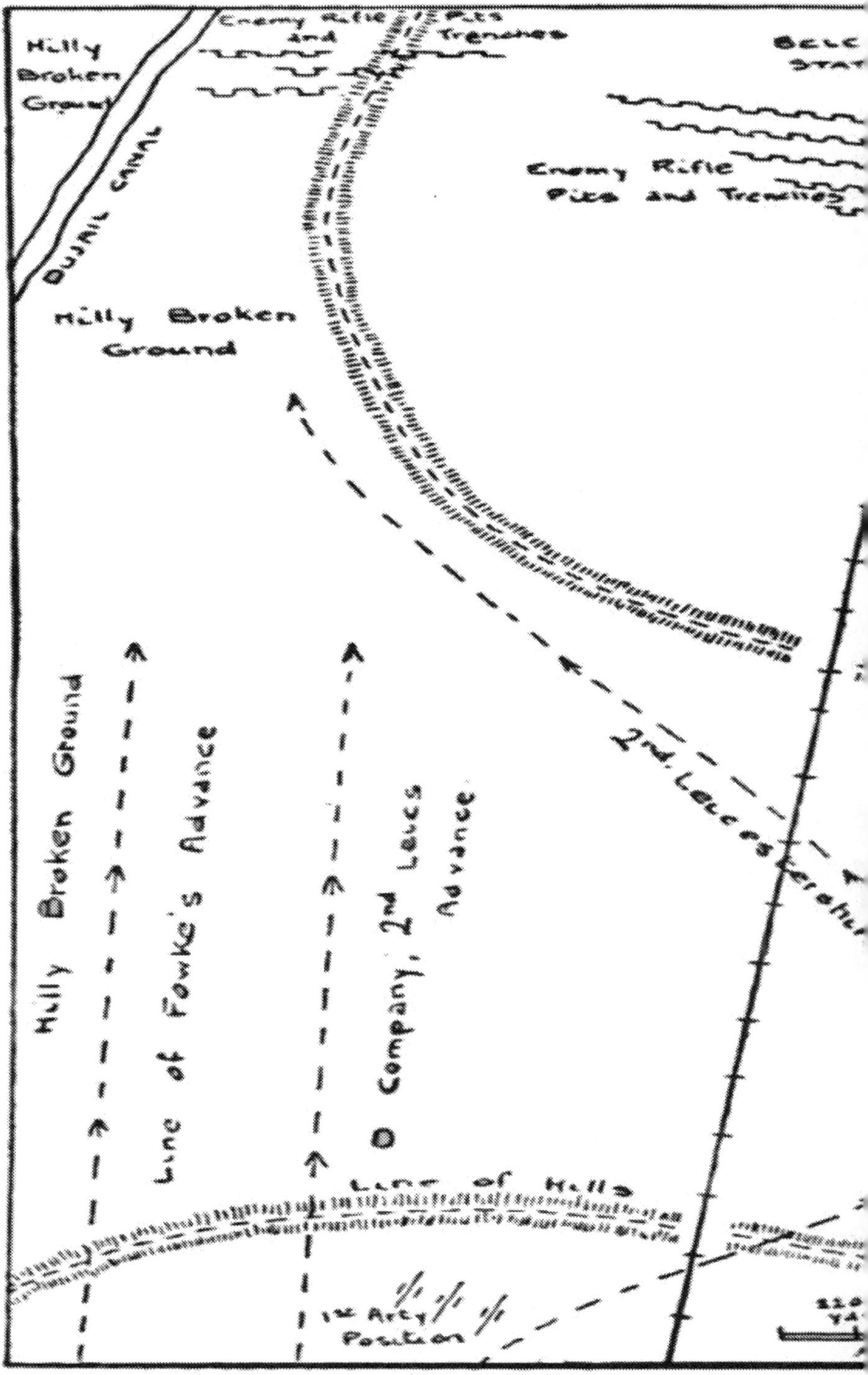

Hilly Broken Ground
Enemy Rifle Pits and Trenches
Dujail Canal
Enemy Rifle Pits and Trenches
Hilly Broken Ground
Hilly Broken Ground
Line of Fowke's Advance
Company, 2nd Leics Advance
Line of Hills
1st Arty Position

BELCO
STATION

Broken Hilly
Ground

Enemy Rifle
Pits and Trenches

Last Arty
Position

Railway

Line of Hills

Sims Attack

Verchere's Attack

53rd and 31st

2nd Arty.
Position

220 YDS | ¼ | ½ | 1 Mile

APPROXIMATE SCALE

enemy reinforced the position from his main one at Harbe. He must have had other casualties in addition to our prisoners. Our left wing, when they occupied the hills, saw four or five hundred Turks 'skirr away' in one body, and the machine-gunners found a target. Raiding-parties of Arabs hung on our flanks throughout the day, and increased the force against us, at any rate numerically.

The day had been cloudy and comparatively cool, and an exquisite evening crowned it. With dusk I left the station, where wounded Turks were groaning and shells bursting, and sought the hills. The shrapnel was dying down, and, once off the plain, all was quiet. The scene here was one of great loveliness. The Dujail, a narrow canal from the Tigris, ran swiftly with water of delightful coldness and sweetness. The canal was fringed with flowers, poppies, marguerites, and campions; the innumerable folds and hollows were emerald-green. C Company were holding the extreme left of our picket-line. Here I found Hasted, Hall, Fisher, and Charles Copeman. We held a dry, very deep irrigation-canal, running at right angles to the Dujail. There were no shells, and we could listen composedly to the last of the shrapnel away on the right. The full moon presently flooded the hills with enchantment. But our night was broken by Arab raids. Twice these robbers of the dead and wounded tried to rush us. The first party probably escaped in the bushes, but the second suffered casualties. In the evening Arabs had raided our aid-post, wounding the attendant, who escaped with difficulty. Fortunately there was none but dead there; these they stripped, cutting off one man's finger for the ring on it. All night long they prowled the battlefield and dug up our buried dead. For which, retribution came next day.

Fisher and I scraped a hole in our canal, and tried to sleep. But a cold wind sneaked about the *nulla*, and the hours dragged past with extreme discomfort. No one had blanket or overcoat, and most were in shorts. At dawn we had ten minutes' notice to rejoin the rest of the regiment behind the station. In that ten minutes I had opportunity to admire the soldier-man's resourcefulness. One of the picket, thrusting his hand deep into one of the countless holes in our canal-wall, found two tiny eggs. Raising fat in some fashion—probably a candle-end—he had fried eggs for breakfast before we moved. The eggs were presumed to be grouse-eggs. More likely they were bee-eater's, or may have been snake's or lizard's. These canals are haunted by huge monitors, and there must be tortoises in the Dujail. However, eggs were found, and eggs were eaten.

On picket the men's talk was interesting to hear. They were regardless of the discomfort they had known so long; and when his turn came to watch, every man was eager to lend his waterproof sheet to Fisher and me, who had only our thin khaki. Marner's death had gone deep.

'I hear Mr. Marner's dead,' said a voice.

'I'm sorry to hear that,' said another; 'he was a nice feller.'

'He was a good feller an' a',' said a third.

'He was more like a brother to me than an officer,' his platoon-sergeant told me.

These were brief tributes to an able and conscientious man, but they sufficed. At Sumaikchah our bivvies had been side by side, where the green was most glowing, and we had rejoiced together in that light and colour.

Beled Station was a small action, scarcely bigger than those dignified in the Boer War with the name of battles. Our casualties were little over a hundred for the whole day, and more than half of these were incurred in the station itself. The Leicestershires lost twenty, three killed among them; several of the wounded died later. But the action attained considerable fame locally as a model of a successful little battle. Our losses were miraculously slight. But for the very great skill with which the two separate attacks were organized, and the constant alertness which exploited every one of the ground's endless irregularities, our losses must have been many times heavier. The advance was conducted with caution and the utmost economy of life; but the moment a breach was effected or an opportunity offered, then there was a lightning blow and a swift push forward. Thus the enemy in the station were trapped before they realized that their retreat was threatened. The careless trooping together at the station was the one regrettable thing, and it cost us dear. The water of Beled Station was like the water brought to David from Bethlehem.

For the action itself, a small force advanced steadily throughout the day, with unreliable maps, over ten miles of broken country, which was admirably furnished with posts of defence, which posts they seized and turned into advantages for attack. They captured a strong position and over two hundred prisoners, three machine-guns, and some hundreds of rifles with less than half the casualties their numerically superior foe sustained. Since a small battle is an epitome of a large one, and far easier to see in detail, even this lengthy account may have justification. The Army Commander's opinion was shown not alone by his congratulatory message, but by the immediate honours awarded. To the Leicestershires fell one Military Cross[4] and four Military Medals, one of the latter going to Sergeant Batten, Marner's platoon-sergeant.

---

[4] Westlake's. See next chapter.

The water-tank leans against the station no longer, and they have repaired the crumbled walls. But the cracks and fissures in the great fort lift eloquent witness to the way both armies desired it, and the quiet, beautiful hills carry their scars also.

*The rushing brook, the silken grass and pride*
*Of poppies burning red where Marner died,*
*Unchanged! and in the station still, as then,*
*The water that was bought with blood of men.*

## Chapter 2
# Harbe

> *Behold, as may unworthiness define,*
> *A little touch of Harry in the night.*
> King Henry V
>
> *If I thought Hell was worse than*
> *Mesopotamia, I'd be a good man.*
> Sayings of Fowke

Next morning was one of leisure. The 19th Brigade took up our line, and we bivouacked before the station. We fed and washed and slept. The enemy put a few shells on to the 19th Brigade, doing no damage, and when that Brigade pushed on to Harbe he fell back on his strong lines at Istabulat, another four miles. The 19th Brigade, with only one or two men wounded, seized Harbe and twenty-four railway-trucks, which were of great assistance presently, when the mules drew them along the track with ammunition for the assault on Istabulat.

In the afternoon the 28th Brigade followed to Harbe. The heat was considerable, but the journey was short. Beyond the river plunging shells told us that our troops were pushing up both banks of the Tigris simultaneously.

The 21st Brigade took over Beled. With them remained the Cherub, wielding for one day the flaming sword of retribution. Arabs had desecrated our graves as they always did, and had stripped our dead. The Cherub put the bodies back and dug several dummy graves. In these last he put Mills bombs; removing the pin, he held each bomb down as the earth was delicately piled over. The deed called for great nerve; he could feel the bomb quick to jump under his finger's pressure. Arabs watched impudently, sniping his party from a few hundred yards away. Neither did they let him get more than a quarter of a mile away, when he had finished, before they flocked down. The Cherub made his way to the station, and watched, as a boy watches a bird-trap. The Arabs fell to scooping out the soil badger-fashion with their hands. There was an explosion, and the earth shot up in a fountain of clods. The robbers ran, but returned immediately and carried off two of their number, casualties. Then they remained to dig. Colonel Leslie, commanding the 21st Brigade, had watched from Beled Station with enthusiasm, and he now turned a machine-gun on them. The Cherub, returning to the scene of his labours, found that the Arabs had dug two feet deeper than his original grave, breaking up the stiff ground with their fingers. To these desperate people a piece of cloth seemed cheap at the cost of two dead or wounded.

From first to last nothing moved deeper anger than their constant exhumation of our dead, and murder, for robbery's sake, of the wounded or isolated. Major Harley, A.P.M. of Baghdad in later days, learnt to admire the ability of the Arabs, whose brief Golden Age, when Abbasids ruled, so far outshone contemporary Europe. When he pressed them on their ghoul-like ways, they replied, 'You

British are so foolish. You bury the dead with the clothes. The dead do not need clothes, and we do.'

The logic of this does not carry far. To them, as Mussulmans, graves were sacrosanct to a unique degree; a suspicion of disrespect on our part would rouse the whole of Islam to flaming wrath. They were criminals, by their own ethos, when they desecrated our dead. Moreover, they murdered whenever they could, in the cruellest and beastliest fashion. The marvel is, our actions of reprisal were so rare. Apart from this of the Cherub's, only two came within my personal knowledge. Of these two cases, one I and nearly the whole division considered savage and unjustifiable, which was also the official view. It was the act of a very young subaltern, mistakenly interpreting an order. In the other case an Arab was caught red-handed, lurking in a ditch on our line of march, with one of their loaded knobkerries for any straggler. I do not know what happened, but have no doubt that he was shot.

It cannot be said that they acted for patriotic motives, as the Spanish guerrillas against Napoleon's troops. I remember an article[5] by Sir William Willcocks dealing with his experiences before the war, in which he tells how he and a friend went ashore from a steamer on the Tigris. An Arab calmly dropped on one knee and took aim at the Englishmen, as if the latter were gazelles or partridges. He missed, and they followed him into his village, where they asked him why he had fired. The man answered that he did it in self-defence, for the others had fired first.

'That,' said the Englishmen, 'is impossible, for you see we are unarmed.'

---

[5] 'Two and a Half Years in Mesopotamia,' Blackwood's Magazine March, 1916.

Hearing this, the village rushed on them and robbed them of their valuables. Yet one of them was an official high in Government service.

The other side of the shield, as it affected Brother Buddu, was shown next day at Harbe. At dawn three men and four women were found in the middle of the 19th Brigade's camp, outside General Peebles' tent, wailing. The women said their husbands had been bayoneted and mutilated by Turks a fortnight before, and buried here. This story proved true. The women dug up and bore off the decomposing fragments for decent burial.

The Buddu was an alien in his own land, loathed and oppressed by the Turk. In his turn he robbed and slew as chance offered. He pursued the chase for the pelt, and went after human life as our more civilized race go after buck.

About this time the Bishop of Nagpur was on his second visit from India. His see was usually mispronounced as Nankipoo. He was following us up to consecrate the graves of our battlefields. Great delight was given by the thought that Westlake's still unexploded bombs would receive consecration also for any retributive work that awaited them. And we brooded over the suggestion that the good Bishop might find, even in Mesopotamia, Elijah's way to heaven, fiery-chariot-wise.

Our new camp was amid mounds and ruins. We found green coins, pottery fragments, and shells with very lovely mother-of-pearl. The Dujail ran near by, and made a green streak through an arid waste. The whole landscape seemed one dust-heap, sand and rubbish. But by the brook were poppies, marguerites, delicate pink campions, wheat and barley growing as weeds of former cultivation, and thickets of blue-flowered liquorice. There were many thorns, especially a squat shrub with white papery globes. A large and particularly fleshy broom-rape, recently flowering, festered unpleasantly everywhere.

April was well on, and the sun gained power daily. The camp had a thousand discomforts. We lay under bivvies formed of a blanket, supported on a rifle and held down uncertainly by stones. Blinding dust-storms careered over the desert. These djinns, with their whirling sand-robes, would swoop down and whisk the poor shelters away. If the courts above take note of blasphemy under such provocation, the Recording Angel's office was hard worked these days. One would be reading a letter, already wretched enough with heat and flies, and suddenly you would be fighting for breath and sight in a maelstrom of dirt, indescribably filthy dirt, whilst your papers flew up twenty feet and your rifle hit you cruelly over the head. As a Marian martyr observed to an enthusiast who thrust a blazing furze-bush into his face, 'Friend, have I not harm enough? What need of that?' One storm at Harbe blew all night, having made day intolerable and meals out of the question. As Fowke curled himself miserably under his blanket for the night, I heard him deliver himself of the opinion quoted at the head of this chapter.

Flies may be taken for granted. They swarm in these vile relics of old habitation. Moreover, there had been a Turkish camp at hand. But snakes and scorpions were found also almost hourly. The snakes were small asps; the scorpions were small also, but sufficiently painful. My batman was consumed with curiosity as to what a scorpion was like; he had 'heard tell of them' in Gallipoli. The listening Gods took account of his desire, and he was mildly stung the day we left.

We spent the best part of a fortnight at Harbe. Morning and evening were enlivened by regular hates. So we had to dig trenches. But there were more memorable happenings at Harbe than the discomforts. Hebden returned with stores of sorts from Baghdad. Two new subalterns, Sowter and Keely, came. On Tuesday Hall's M.C. for Sannaiyat was announced. We celebrated this with grateful hymn far into night. Thursday brought the Cherub's M.C., another very popular honour, and we sang again, and the mules from their mess sang a chorus back, as before.

> *When as at dusk our Mess carouse,*
> *With catches strong and brave,*
> *The mules their tuneful hearts arouse,*
> *And answer stave for stave.*
> *'Dumb nature' breaks in festive noise,*
> *Remembering in this East*
> *The mystic bond which knits the joys*
> *Of righteous man and beast.*
> *Then pass the flowing bowl about—*
> *Our stores have come to-day—*
> *And let the youngest captain shout,*
> *And let the asses bray.*
> *The thorny trudge awhile forget,*
> *And foeman's waiting host!*
> *To-morrow bomb and bayonet—*
> *To-night we keep the toast!*

These light-hearted evenings seemed, even then, sacramental. We were waiting while the Third Corps and the cavalry cleared the other bank of the Tigris, level with us. On the 19th the river was bridged at Sinijah, which made close touch between the two corps possible and passage of men and guns. About the same time the cavalry captured twelve hundred and fifty Turks on the Shat-el-Adhaim. Our wait was necessary. But we knew the enemy was terribly entrenched less than six miles away, and that our sternest fight since Sannaiyat was preparing. 'This will be a full-dress affair, with the corps artillery,' I was told. Some of my comrades were under twenty; others, like Fowke and Grant-Anderson, were men of ripe age and experience in many lands. But all had aged in spirit. Hall, though his years were only nineteen, had grown since Sannaiyat into a man, responsibility touching his old gaiety with power. So we waited on this beach of conflict.

One evening stands out by its beauty and unconscious greatness. It happened thus. Remember how young many were, and it is small wonder if depression came at times. After the trying trench warfare before Kut had come the rush to Baghdad, a period of strain and tremendous effort. We had been fighting and marching continuously for many weeks, with every discomfort and over a cursed monotonous plain, without even the palliation of fairly regular mails. When men have been 'going over the top' repeatedly, emerging always with comrades gone, the nerves give way. We longed to be at that Istabulat position. Yet here we had to wait while Cailley's Column fought level with us, and day by day those sullen lines were strengthening. We had barely six thousand men to throw at them. So one night talk became discontented, and some one wished some reinforcement could be with us from the immense armies which our papers bragged were being trained at home. Then another—G.A. or Fowke—replied:

*Oh that we now had here*
*But one ten thousand of those men in England*
*That do no work to-day!*

Swiftly that immortal scene, of the English spirit facing great odds invincibly, followed, passage racing after passage.

*God's will! I pray thee, wish not one man more!*

It was an electric spark. I never heard poetry, or literature at all, mentioned save this once. But all were eager and speaking, for all had read Henry V. When the lines were reached,

> *Rather proclaim it, Westmorland, through my host,*
> *That he which hath no stomach to this fight,*
> *Let him depart,*

laughter cleansed every spirit present of fear, and the shadow of fear, misgiving. Nothing less grimly humorous than the notion of such an offer being made now, or of the alleged consequences of such an offer, in the instant streaming away of all His Majesty's Forces in Mesopotamia, could have made so complete a purgation. Comedy took upon herself the office of Tragedy. When voices could rise above the laughter, they went on:

> *His passport shall be made,*
> *And crowns for convoy put into his purse.*

'Movement-orders down the line and ration-indents,' was the emendation.

> *We would not die in that man's company*
> *That fears his fellowship to die with us.*

And Fowke's voice towered to an ecstasy of sarcasm as he assured his unbelieving hearers that

> *Gentlemen in England, now abed,*
> *Shall think themselves accursed they were not here.*

As a Turkish attack was considered possible, every morning we stood-to for that 'witching hour,' immediately before dawn, which is usually selected for 'hopping the parapet.' The brigades reconnoitred, and exchanged shots with enemy pickets. Fritz came, of course. Then the 19th Brigade went on, and took up a position two miles in front behind the Median Wall, of which more hereafter. The battle preparations went busily forward.

Our camp was strewn with pebbles, an old shingle-beach, for we were on the ancient edges of the sea, before the river had built up Iraq.[6] The stones at Beled had been the first signs that we were off the alluvial plain. South of Baghdad it was reported that a reward of £100 would be paid (by whom I never heard) to the finder of any sort of stone. And now, after our long sojourn in stoneless lands, these pebbles were a temptation, and there was a deal of surreptitious chucking-about. One watched with secret glee while a smitten colleague pretended to be otherwise occupied, but nevertheless kept cunning eyes searching for the offender. I enjoyed myself best, for I lay and watched the daily parade of the troops before breakfast, and could inquire genially, 'Have you had a good stand-to?'

Fowke asked the wastes in a soaring falsetto, 'Why do the heathen rage?' And he was returned question for question, with 'Why do you keep laughing at me with those big, blue eyes?' Then the camp would rock with song as we fell to shaving and, after, breakfast.

The superstitions which old experience had justified waxed strong as the days went by. When McInerney marked out a quoits-court and Charles Copeman dug a mess—these officers found their amusement in singular ways, and would have been hurt had any one attempted to usurp their self-appointed duties—and when I put in services for Sunday, the 22nd, it was recognized that we should march, and fight on the Sabbath. Not more anxiously did the legionary listen for tales of supernatural fires in the corn and of statues sweating blood than the regiments asked each other, 'Have you dug a mess yet? Has

---

[6] South Mesopotamia; north is Jezireh.

the padre put in services?' Two of us went down with colitis—possibly the Sumaikchah waters were not even yet done with—and Fowke, as they left us, profaned Royal Harry's words:

*He which hath no stomach to this fight,*
*Let him depart.*

For all this, Shakespeare had a share in the storming of Istabulat, as will be seen; as the ghost of Bishop Adhemar, who had died at Antioch, was said to have gone before Godfrey of Boulogne's scaling-ladder when the Crusaders took Jerusalem. ('Thank God!' said they. 'He was not frustrate of his vows.')

On Friday rain came, and Charles Copeman, who had, as already indicated, a passion for digging—caught, perchance, in boyhood from his father's sexton—dug a funk-hole from the enemy shell-fire. McInerney helped him. Now this was not an ordinary funk-hole. It was a very splendid and elaborate hole, and no one was allowed to come near, lest he cause its perfection to crumble away. So, to dry ourselves after the rain, we all dug, and the Desert-Gods laughed in their bitter little minds as they saw. Among the rest, Sowter and I dug a hole, dug deeply, widely, with much laughter and joyfulness. And to us, as the afternoon wore towards evening, came the C.O., and, after watching us for a few minutes, told us that we marched in an hour.

# Chapter 3
# The First Battle of Istabulat

*These men, the steadfast among spears, dying, won for themselves a crown of glory that fadeth not away.*

Greek Anthology

In the quiet light we crossed the railway, and moved up to the Median Wall, in all a march of perhaps a mile and a half. This wall was old in Xenophon's time[7]; and along its northern side his army moved, watching, and watched by, the troops of Tissaphernes, moving parallel on the other side. He speaks of it as twenty feet in breadth and one hundred feet in height. Once it was the border between Assyria and Babylonia, and must have stretched to the Euphrates. Even now it runs from the Tigris far into the desert. It has crumbled to one-third of the height given by Xenophon. The semblance of a wall no longer, it is a mighty flank of earth, covering tiers of bricks. It effectually hid our movements as we crossed the plain before it. The Turk was shrapnelling the wall and its approaches, endeavouring to reply to some howitzers. These last we left on our right. As I happened to be the nearest officer,

---
[7] Anabasis, Book ii.

the major came up and asked me that the Leicestershires should move more to the left, in case any of his guns had a premature.

We fell silently into our places behind the wall. The artillery behind us were favoured with a certain amount of *zizyph*-scrub; but the wall furnished no cover but itself. Fowke, who at all times indulged in a great deal of gloomy prognostication, known as 'Fowke-lore,' and received with delight, but not quite implicit belief, foretold that on the morrow our cavalry—it was a point of principle with the infantry to assume that the cavalry, as well as all Higher Commands, were capable of every stupidity and of nothing but stupidity—would cut up B Company, his own, who had a certain unattractive duty assigned to them on the extreme left. He also told us that the Median Wall would be shelled to blazes, which seemed pretty probable.

The clearest figure in my memory for this hurried, stealthy evening is J.Y. Copeman, cousin of Charles. 'J.Y.'—for he never carried any graver appellation than mere initials—once a rising lawyer in Vancouver, was now our quartermaster. The gayest and most debonair figure in the division, known and popular everywhere, he was also an incredibly efficient quartermaster. Possibly the same qualities make for success in law and quartermastering. His gaiety was the mask for a most unsleeping energy and very great ability. He was once dubbed, by a person more alliterative than observant, 'a frail, flitting figure with a fly-flap.' Yet he had taken over Brodie's job, at Sannaiyat, when that experienced 'quarter' had wakened suddenly to find that an aeroplane bomb had wounded him. Within a year of this event I was privileged to be present at an argument between our D.A.D.O.S. and our D.A.D.S. & T.,[8]

---

[8] The Divisional Heads of Ordnance and Supply and Transport.

as to whether Copeman or Jock Reid, of the Seaforths, was the greater quartermaster. Where two such authorities failed to come to a decision, I must stand aside, especially as both J.Y. and Reid are my friends. With his ability J.Y. had an indomitable resolve, which made him refuse to go sick. He carried on through months of constant ill-health; sometimes he was borne on one of his own ration-carts, too unwell to walk or ride. He fed alone, but had a familiar, in the shape of a ridiculously clever and most selfish cat. And it is J.Y. whom I remember on this eve of Istabulat—J.Y. marshalling his carts swiftly and silently up to the wall when darkness had fallen, and J.Y. next morning scurrying them away before dawn.

A Company went on picket, B and C patrolled before our lines, D lay behind the wall. Fires were kept low. J.Y. got our blankets up to us, and we had some sleep.

Next day, the 21st, all kit was packed and on the carts by 4 a.m. Breakfast was at 3.30; hot tea and a slice of bacon. The second line fell back. Then we clung to the wall, and waited; all but Fowke. That warrior moved off to the left with part of B Company, all carrying spades. Their task was to come out of the shelter of the wall as soon as the action began, and to work their spades frantically, sending up such dust-clouds that the bemused Turk might suppose a new Army Corps advancing to attack his right, and take steps accordingly. The brown-coated figure took a sombre farewell of me, reminding us that, though his crowd were going to be cut up by our own cavalry, the rest of us would be shelled into annihilation when Johnny opened on the famous wall. 'He's bound to have the exact range, for it's such a landmark. Besides, he's got German archaeologists with him, who've dug here for years and years; they know every brick. And he's been practising on it for weeks. You saw how he had it last night when we came up.'

The two actions which it is customary to call the two Battles of Istabulat were fought in positions some miles apart. The title of Istabulat, or of Dujail River, may fitly be reserved for the first action. The action of the 22nd may then be known as that of Istabulat Mounds. The Istabulat fight was one in which my own Brigade were spectators, except for isolated and piece-meal action. We were in reserve; and the 8th Brigade, of the 3rd Division, were in support, in line with us, and behind the Median Wall. The enemy were trying a new bowler, Shefket Pasha being in command, vice Kazim Karabekir Bey, who had resigned from command of their Eighteenth Corps just before Baghdad fell. We should not have supposed that this made any difference, even had we known.

The Istabulat battle has been described in print,[9] though inadequately and, in one important respect, most unfairly. That unfairness I shall correct in the next chapter. But for this first action I do not propose to do more than give an outline of the work of the two Brigades engaged, and an account of our own part in reserve.

The enemy's position was of immense strength. Old mounds made an upraised plateau, through which the Dujail Canal ran swiftly between steep and lofty banks. The 19th and 21st Brigades attacked in converging columns, the first thrusting right in, the second coming with an arm sweep round. Thus, both frontal and flank attacks were provided. The enemy's position was so strong, his redoubts so lofty, and the whole formidable terrain had been so entrenched and wired round that I do not believe

---

[9] 'The Battle that Won Samarrah,' by Brigadier-General A.G. Wauchope, C.M.G., D.S.O.; Blackwood's, April, 1918.

we hoped to do more than eat our way into a part of his line. The operation was magnificent bluff. His morale was calculated to be now so low that he was likely to evacuate the position if we bit deeply into it. If this view is correct, General Maude was taking a heavy risk. But he not only always made all preparation possible before he struck, but on occasion did not hesitate to strike where the odds should have been against success, but the prize of success was great, and the morale of the troops against him weakened by repeated blows. In the Jebel Hamrin his calculation failed. But at Istabulat it succeeded. But, had the Turk been as he was in Sannaiyat days, two months back, we should have had a week of dreadful fighting instead of one bloody day. Holding Istabulat heights was a force estimated at seven thousand four hundred infantry and five hundred sabres, with thirty-two guns. This force, in its perfect position, we attacked with two weak brigades.

The carts had scuttled away; J.Y. and his cat had stalked off through the dimness. We were shivering behind the wall. At 5 a.m. the bombardment opened. From five to seven we brought every gun to bear on the enemy. Istabulat, like the last of Sannaiyat's five battles, was an artillery battle, in the sense that the infantry, less strongly and splendidly supported, would have been helpless. 'I'll never say a word against the gunners again after to-day and Sannaiyat,' said a wounded Seaforths' officer to me in the evening. The field-guns were well up from the start, and the 'hows' soon advanced. When the action began, the latter were half-a-mile behind us at the wall. It was an impressive sight, the smoke rushing out with each discharge, and then swaying back with the gun's recoil. But the guns were rarely stationary long, and we soon had the unwonted experience of finding ourselves well behind our own artillery. Finally, in places our batteries were firing at almost point-blank range; the enemy was simply blasted out of his trenches.

Fowke's dust-up drew a few shells; and the Turk strengthened his right to meet this new threat. But presently Fritz came over, very low and very impudent. He reported that it was only Fowke, and sheered off with a contempt quite visible from the ground. He was so low that we fired at him with rifles, vainly; then he went, and was swooping down on the Seaforths' attack and machine-gunning it.

The 19th Brigade got their first objectives with very few casualties. But then the enemy poured a murderous fire on to them from every sort of weapon. The 21st Brigade all but accomplished their impossible task. At a critical point a terrible misfortune occurred. The 9th Bhopals—who were playfully and better known as the 9th 'Bo-Peeps'—crossed in front of a strong machine-gun position instead of outflanking it. The Turks held their fire till the regiment was close up. The latter lost two hundred men in three minutes; and a large body of Turks, who were wavering on the edge of surrender, fell back instead. The Bhopals never recovered from this disaster. The skeleton of a battalion which survived the fight was sent down the line, and its place taken by the 1st Guides from India.

Two other battalions of the 21st Brigade, the 2nd Black Watch and the 1/8th Gurkhas, crossed a plain bare of cover. They crossed at terrible cost, and scaled the all but sheer walls of the Turkish left. But it was too much; and a counter-attack swept the survivors off, and took two officers and several men prisoners. Evening found our forces held, though the whole enemy front line was ours and our teeth were fixed deeply into the position. The Black Watch had lost all four company commanders, killed.

It is not possible to convey to paper the heroism and agony of this day. Mackenzie, of the Seaforths, who won the D.S.O. two months previously at Sannaiyat for valour which in any previous war would have won the V.C., was shot dead as he was offering his water-bottle to a wounded Turk. Irvine, of the 9th Bhopals, was wounded, and lay out all day; two wounded Turks looked after him, surrendering when we ultimately came up. The Gurkhas and Bhopals took two hundred and thirty prisoners. A Black Watch private captured nine Turks and brought them in, himself supporting the last of the file, who was wounded. A machine-gunner, isolated when his comrades were killed or driven back, although wounded, worked his gun till we advanced again.

The artillery, as was inevitable from the role they filled, suffered. Major the Earl of Suffolk, commanding B/56th Battery, was killed by shrapnel through the heart. He was a popular, unassuming man. Lieutenant Stewart, of the same battery, was wounded. Colonel Cotter, commanding the 56th Brigade, R.F.A., was hit in the forehead. Lieutenant Hart's wrist was shot through. The 14th Battery had two hundred 5.9's burst round them; yet they brought up their team, one by one, and got the guns away, losing men, but no animals.

Meanwhile from the Median Wall the 'Tigers'[10] watched the fight. One could not help being reminded of the grand-stand at a football match. Sitting on the further side and below the crest, the officers watched the Indians pushing over the plain steadily through heavy shelling. We saw dreadful pounding away on our left, where 5.9's plunged and burst among the trenches the Seaforths

---

[10] The Leicestershires' badge is a tiger, commemorating service in India a century ago.

were holding. Yet even a battle grows monotonous; so in the afternoon we went down to the trenches before the wall to rest, so far as heat and flies would permit. In that period of slackness a number of men swarmed up the wall. Instead of sitting where we had done, they sat on the crest, against the sky-line. Hitherto the shrapnel had not come nearer than a ridge four hundred yards away, which had been often and well peppered. But now came the hateful whistle, and the ridge was swept from end to end with both H.E. and shrapnel. In our trenches we were spattered with pebbles. Thorpe, next to me, got a piece of H.E. in his coat. But we escaped a direct hit. One shell passing overhead skimmed the ridge and burst on the other side, scattering Colonel Knatchbull's kit and smashing his fishing-rod. It killed a groom and wounded three other men, and wounded three horses so badly that they all had to be killed. It is always men on duty, holding horses or otherwise unable to escape, who pay for the curiosity of the idle.

Firing continued very heavy till dusk. In the evening I buried the man killed by the shell, and then went back to find the clearing-station. Part of a padre's recognized function is to cull and purvey news. And I had many friends engaged. A couple of miles back I found the 7th British Field Ambulance, to which my own chief, A.E. Knott, was attached. The sight here was far more nerve-racking than a battlefield. It was an open human shambles, with miserable men lying about, some waiting on tables to be operated on. Knott was about to help in amputating a leg. In the few words I had with him I learnt that Suffolk was killed. I think I am right when I say that he was the only man killed among our 7th Division gunners. (We had other artillery with us, and they lost heavily.) It seemed strangely mediaeval, as from the days of Agincourt or Creçi, that Death, scarring so many, but forbearing to exact their uttermost, should strike down so great a name and one that is written on so many pages of our history. I knew well how many would mourn the man. I asked Knott the question of questions, 'What are our casualties?' These, one knew, must be heavy; but I was appalled by his reply, 'Sixteen hundred to one o'clock.'

I left the wretched scene and went back. Part of the way McLeod, of the Seaforths, his right arm in a sling, wandered with me, talking dazedly of the day and its fortunes. I found an officer with whom I had travelled on a river-boat not long before, when his mind held the presentiment of death in his first action. He, like McLeod, went out from Istabulat with the card, 'G.S.[11] wound, right arm.' So much for presentiment in some cases. A different case occurred next day.

I found my mess sitting down to dinner. 'Montag' Warren, our P.M.C., had excellently acquired dates and white mulberries, which last made a stew, poorly tasting, but a change from long monotony. A clamour greeted me. 'Where've you been, padre? What's the news?' I told them we had got on well. Then some one asked, 'But what did you hear about our casualties?' Minds were tense, for every one knew that next day our brigade must take up the attack, and for a whole day we had seen Hell in full eruption on our right. I told them other things I had learnt—told them anything that might brush aside the awkward question. But they demanded to know. Neither do I see how I could have avoided telling. So at last I said, 'Well, what I was told was sixteen hundred.'

---

[11] Gun-shot.

Silence fell. To some, sixteen hundred may seem a butcher's bill so trifling that brave men—and these were men superlatively brave, officers of the 17th Foot, and some of them had seen more pitched battles than years, had known Ypres and Loos and Neuve Chapelle, Gallipoli and Sheikh Saad—would not concede it a momentary blanching of the cheek. But these sixteen hundred casualties were out of barely four thousand men engaged, including gunners. In that minute each man communed with his own spirit,

*Voyaging through strange fields of thought alone.*

The reader will be weary of Henry V. Nevertheless Shakespeare came to the aid of us, his countrymen, again as gallant old Fowke quoted from the heart and brain of England:

*He which hath no stomach to this fight,*
*Let him depart....*
*We would not die in that man's company,*
*That fears his fellowship to die with us.*

So laughter ended a terrible day. Next day our tiny band was the spearhead of a handful of fifteen hundred bayonets, who caught the Turk in his fastnesses, wrested guns and prisoners from him, and slew and broke his forces so that they recoiled for thirty miles.

There was no rest. Through the darkness J.Y. flitted to and fro, and here and there a spectral blaze flickered furtively. We had neither blankets nor greatcoats, for fear of shell-fire made it impossible to bring the carts up. The night was infernal with cold; sand-flies rose in myriads from the ground; we shivered and itched in our shorts. Old aches and pains found me out, rheumatism and troubles of a tropical climate. I lay between two men, both of whom had seen their last sunset; one was Sergeant-Major Whatsize. Infinitely far off seemed peace and the time, as Grant-Anderson expressed it,

> *When the Gurkhas cease from gurkhing, and the Sikhs are sick no more.*

At midnight came a roar, then a crashing. It was Johnny blowing up Istabulat Station. At three o'clock we were aroused.

## Chapter 4
# The Battle for Samarra

*Salute the sacred dead,*
*Who went and who return not.*

J.R. Lowell

Day was welcome, for it brought movement, though movement harassed by cold and then by heat and ever-increasing clouds of flies. We snatched our mugs of tea, our bread and bacon. At 3.30 we moved off. We marched behind the wall, then crossed the Dujail, and pushed towards the left flank of the enemy's position. Vast clouds of white dust shut us close from any knowledge as we climbed up a narrow pass. Fortunately the light was hardly even dim yet.

We dropped into a plain, and saw the Hero's Way by which the others had gone. Dead Gurkhas and Highlanders lay everywhere. I have always felt that the sight of a dead Highlander touches even deeper springs of pathos than the sight of any other corpse. Analysed, the feeling comes to this, I think: in his kilt he seems so obviously a peasant, lying murdered on the breast of the Universal Mother.

So we marvelled as we saw the way and the way's price—marvelled that any could have survived to that stiff, towering redoubt, with its moat of trenches and the trenches ringing its sides; and marvelled most of all that any should have scaled its top, though for a moment only. These trenches held abundant dead, Turks and our own. On the reverse slope I came on rows of the enemy, huddled on their knees, their hands lifted to shield their heads from the shrapnel which had killed them. Below ran Dujail in its steep ditch; inland the plateau rose, against which the 19th Brigade had surged.

For once the Turk's retreat had been precipitate. That master of rearguard warfare had meant to stand here, to save railhead and all its rolling-stock. His dead were more than ours; and all our way was strewn with debris. Candles and cones of sugar were in plenty, ammunition, blankets—for Johnny had not been cold, as we had—bivvies, clothes, slippers. I carried an ammunition-box a few miles, thinking it would make a good letter-case.

The enemy had gone. Before passing to tell of this new day's battle I quote, from Hasted's[12] account, a description of Istabulat lines:

> The Turks intended to spend the summer there; they did not contemplate an attack before the hot weather set in. Three well-concealed lines of trenches had been prepared, on small hills and amongst deep *nullas*, with the water-supply of the Dujail running through the centre. Advanced redoubts and strong points made the defences formidable.
>
> The brigade formed up about 6.30 a.m., the 53rd Sikhs coming in from picket on the extreme right. We passed the 56th Brigade, R.F.A., whose officers eagerly came with us a short distance, telling us of the previous day. We halted for breakfast.

---

[12] A lecture delivered by him at Rawal Pindi, India. See Preface.

Verbal orders came from Division. They were just 'Push on vigorously.' With it was coupled an assurance that there was nothing against us, that the enemy was fleeing, thoroughly demoralized.

We moved on. From across the Tigris guns boomed steadily. Distant glimpses of river showed shoals, islands, spaces green with cultivation. An enemy plane, reconnoitring, was shot down, and pilot and observer killed. This incident had an important influence on the battle which followed. Even at this stage of the campaign, we fought in Mesopotamia, both sides, with the most exiguous number of planes. The Turks having lost their best machine and pilot, our old friend Fritz, feared to risk another. Hence, when the mounds of the ancient city of Istabulat lay across our front, the hostile observation was from the ground in front and from our left flank only. And we were enabled to pass through a depression, whilst his fire went overhead, and so into the mounds.

We passed a 5.9 disabled by a direct hit and nearly buried. The bare country was cracked with *nullas*, some of them deep. Then we opened into artillery formation, and entered utter desert. In front were innumerable mounds, a dead town of long ago. We went warily, with that quiet expectation, almost the hardest of all experiences to endure, of the first shell's coming. The official message was that the enemy was incapable of serious opposition. But of this the rank and file knew nothing; had they known, old experience would have made them sceptical. Fowke's view, that all would prove to be for the worst in the worst of all possible worlds and arrangements, was the reigning philosophy. An adapted edition of Schopenhauer would have sold well in the mess (or anywhere in Mesopotamia). Novelists speak of the hero being conscious that eyes, in

Turkish G...

Turkish Trenches

Turkish Trench

2nd Lei...
D. Co.   A. C...
Second M...
5bn. Rifles

Turkish Trenches

RAILWAY
SAMARRAH-BAGHDAD

Ruins of A...
of Ista...

Wilson's
First Aid ✚
Post

/ Indian
/ Cavalry

28th Bde

6bn
R.F.

0   ¼   ½
SCALE

Guns

Leicesters

A. Co.   B. Co.    × Police Post

Well

Leics HQ
· C. Co.

Ancient City
stabulat.

5th. Bde
R F A

Bde. HQ    53rd and
           51st Sikhs

Bde.
F A

1 Mile

TIGRIS RIVER

N

the forest or in his room at night (as may be), are watching, watching. This knowledge governs the feeling of 'going in artillery formation,' with the added knowledge that, though in broad sun, you cannot hope to see your foe, who is certain to spring on you, and merely waits till you are well under fire.

The bolt fell. About 9 a.m. a double report was heard; then the Cherub sent back word, 'Four enemy snipers retiring.' By 9.30 firing was heavy. The Cherub was wounded, and his two scouts killed. The enemy was invisible, and mirage made ranging impossible. The ground four hundred yards away was a fairyland that danced and glimmered. When a target was perceived, of Turks racing back, the orders for fire were changed quickly, from 'Three hundred yards' to 'fourteen hundred yards.' Very vainly. This mirage continued throughout the fight. Ahead was what we called the 'Second Median Wall,' a crumbled wall some twenty feet high, which ran across the front of the mounds. To its extreme left, our right, and in front of this wall, was the Turkish police-post of Istabulat, by which the battle was presently to be raging.

In those mounds the enemy had excellent cover. Our leading company followed the scouts, and took possession of the ruins. The 'Tigers' were arranged in four lines, according to companies, with less than three hundred yards between the lines. Dropping bullets fell fast, especially in the rear lines. About 10 a.m. two shells burst about a hundred yards in front of Wilson and myself. Then Hell opened all her mouths and spat at us. The battalion lay down and waited. Twelve-pounder 'pipsqueaks' came in abundance, with a sprinkling of heavier stuff. Many soldiers prefer the latter. You can hear a 5.9 coming, and it gives you time to collect yourself, and thus perhaps escape giving others the trouble to collect what is left of you. I remember once hearing General Peebles say that in his long experience of many wars he had known only three men absolutely devoid of fear, 'Smith and Brown and—Jones' (mentioning a notorious and most-admired fire-eating brigadier, a little man in whom bursting shells produced every symptom of intoxication except inability to get about). Then he added, 'I'm not sure about Jones.'

It is interesting to notice the different ways in which nervousness shows. I remember one man in whom was never observed the slightest emotion amid the terriblest happenings, till one day some one noticed that whenever he went forward he turned up his jacket-collar, as if to shelter from that fiery rain. Myself, I hate the beginning of conflict, and am eager to push well into it and under the shell-barrage. As there is said to be a cool core in the heart of flame, so there is a certain cool centre for the spirit where horror is radiating out to a wide circumference. In the depths one must surrender one's efforts and trust to elemental powers and agonies, but in the shallows all the calls are on the 'transitory being' whose flesh and blood are pitted against machinery. How can the nerves and trembling thought bear up? Yet they have borne up, even in men quick with sense and imagination. I felt restless as we lay on the flat desert listening to the bullets singing by or to a nosecap's leisured search for a victim, dipping and twisting to left and right till at last it thudded down. If one must lie still, then company gives a feeling of security. Fate may have, doubtless has, a special down on you, but even Fate is unlikely to blow you to bits if the act involves blowing to bits several of her more favoured sons. So I remember with amusement my vague vexation with the curiosity that always made my companion get up and stroll about when under fire, peering round. Though he went scarcely five yards, it seemed like desertion.

We watched our guns run up to the 'Pimple,' a recently built-up mound slightly ahead of us, lately used as a Turkish O. Pip, now accruing to us for the same purpose. The infantry assumed that these wagons and limbers moving a hundred yards to our right would draw all the enemy's fire, in which case we, helpless on the flat, would be shelled out of this existence. But this did not happen; why, I cannot guess, unless I have correctly traced the reason for that bad observation so marked in the Turkish gunning all through this day. We were in the slightest possible depression, with a scarcely perceptible lift on our left and a steady rise before. Shells plunged incessantly down our left, and went whistling far beyond us. But comparatively few burst among us; and the shrapnel burst far too high to do damage.

Our batteries were in position at the 'Pimple.' We rose, marched through a tornado of noise, right-turned, and went across the muzzle of our own guns, also in full blast. In front I saw lines of Leicestershires scaling the slope and melting into the mounds.

My diary notes: 'Men's delight to see river.' We came suddenly upon Brother Tigris, basking in beautiful sunlight, becalmed in bays beneath lofty bluffs. In this dreadful land water meant everything; we had had experiences of thirst, not to be effaced in a lifetime. Away from the river men grew uneasy. The river meant abundance to drink, and bathing; everywhere else water was bad, or the supply precarious. We had been away from the river since that night opposite Sindiyeh. So not the crashing shells, the 'pipsqueaks' ripping the air like dried paper, nor the bullets pinging by, prevented men from greeting so dear a sight. Standing on the beach of imminent strife, in act to plunge, men cried, 'The Tigress, the Tigress!' Instantly a scene flashed back to memory from the book so often near to thought in these days: how Xenophon, weary and anxious with the restlessness and depression of his much-tried troops, heard a clamour from those who had reached a hill-crest, and, riding swiftly up to take measures against the expected peril, found them shouting *'Thalatta, Thalatta.'* Seafaring folk, the most of them, they had caught, far below, their first glimpse of the Euxine, truly a hospitable water to them, since it could bear them home.

Wilson dressed his first wounded in sheltered, broken ground, high above the river. The peaceful beauty of the place is with me still. Above the blue, unruffled pools green flycatchers darted, and rollers spread metallic wings. The left bank lay low and very lovely with flowers and fields. "I will answer you," said Sir Walter Raleigh, asked his opinion of a glass of wine, given as he went to execution, 'as the man did who was going to Tyburn. "This is a good drink, if a man might but tarry by it."' Wilson left me here with Dobson; but almost immediately he sent back asking us to rejoin him. Our few cases, all walking ones, remained in this shelter till such time as they could fall back, and Dobson and I crossed into the mounds.

It was nearly eleven o'clock. Our leading company had advanced by rushes to a distance of a hundred and fifty yards beyond the Second Median Wall. They were within three hundred yards of the main enemy trenches. Battalion Head Quarters was at the wall, the 56th Rifles were to the left, the two Sikh regiments a quarter of a mile to the rear. Machine-gun sections were at the wall, supporting the forward regiments. The 56th Brigade, R.F.A., had moved up, and were firing close behind Wilson's new aid-post. Presently two more companies of Leicestershires were sent beyond the wall, the third in response to a message that the front line had suffered heavily and were short of ammunition. Before the final assault, then, the Leicestershires' line, from the east inland, was D, A, B, these three companies in this order.

But I am anticipating.

Wilson's A.P. was in a dwarf amphitheatre, and was filling up fast. Bullets were zipping over from left and front. The enemy position rested on river and railway, a half-dug position which some six thousand men were frantically completing when we caught them. Away beyond Tigris glittered the golden dome of Samarra mosque; Samarra town and Samarra station, like Baghdad town and station, are on opposite banks of the river. The station was railhead for this finished lower line of eighty miles, and in it were the engines and rolling-stock which had been steadily withdrawn before our advance. Beyond the mounds the ground dropped and stretched, level but broken, swept by machine-gun and rifle, torn with shell and shrapnel, away to Al-Ajik, against Samarra town. Here the Turk resisted savagely. He was ranging on the wall, which was an extremely unhealthy spot, particularly in its gaps, and he enfiladed the mounds from the railway. We flung our fifteen hundred bayonets and our maniple of cavalry at the position. The one British regiment, the Leicestershires, went in three hundred and thirty strong, and lost a hundred and twenty-eight men.

Dropping bullets took toll even before we left the mounds. As I came up to join Wilson a man was carried past. It was Major Adams, acting second-in-command of the 53rd Sikhs. He had gone ahead of his battalion to the wall, where a bullet struck him in the forehead. He died within fifteen minutes, and was unconscious as he went past me. No man in the brigade was more beloved. He was always first to offer hospitality. It was he who met our mess when they first reached Sumaikchah and invited them to come to his own for lunch. I never saw him but with a smile of infinite kindliness on his face, and I saw him very often.

*Face swift to welcome, kindling eyes whose light*
*Saw all as friends, we shall not meet again!*

Here in the aid-post sat the Cherub, struck at last, a flesh-wound in his thigh; with many others. Next to him was Charles Copeman, unwounded, waiting to go forward with his bombers. Presently came Warren, bright and jaunty as a bird, and carrying his left arm. 'I'm all right,' said Montag, 'got a cushy one here.'

On his heels came G.A.; his face was that of a man fresh from the Beatific Vision. Much later, when I had managed to get transport to push him away, I asked him, 'Got your stick, G.A.?' This was a stout stave on which he had carved, patiently and skilfully, his name, 'H.T. Grant-Anderson,' and a fierce and able-looking tiger at the top, then his regiment, then curving round it the names of the actions in which it had supported him: *Sannaiyat, Iron Bridge, Mushaidie, Beled Station*; while down the line now he was to add *Istabulat-Samarra*. This famed work of art he flaunted triumphantly as he climbed into the ambulance.

But with these, and before some of them, came very heavy news. By that fatal wall and on the bullet-swept space before it died many of our bravest. Hall, M.C., aged nineteen, who looked like Kipling's Afridi:

*He trod the ling like a buck in spring, and he looked*
*like a lance in rest;*

Hall fell, facing the finish of our journey and those bright domes of Samarra, already gilded from the sloping sun. His death was merciful, a bullet through the heart; 'and sorrow came, not to him, but to those who loved him.'

The theory was strongly held in the Leicestershires that the only way was to advance steadily. This weakened the enemy's morale, and, further, he had no chance to pick out his ranges accurately. To this theory and practice of theirs they put down the fact that, though in the forefront of all their battles, their losses were often so much slighter than those of units that had acted more cautiously. I quote again from Hasted's brilliant lecture on the battle:

There was no hesitation about the advance. Rushes were never more than twenty yards, more often ten to fifteen yards, as hard as one could go, and as flat as one could lie, at the end of it. The theory, 'the best way of supporting a neighbouring unit is to advance,' was explained at once. The attention of the enemy's rifles and machine-guns was naturally directed to the platoon or section advancing, even when they had completed their rush. Directly one saw a party getting slated, one took advantage of it to advance oneself, in turn drawing fire, but taking care to finish the rush before being properly ranged on. One seldom halted long enough to open covering-fire, and besides, there was nothing to fire at. Despite the very short halt, it is no exaggeration to say that I have seen men go to sleep between the rushes.

Shell-bursts provided excellent cover to advance behind. Individuals, such as runners, adopted a zigzag course with success; we lost very few. Platoons and companies got mixed, but it was not difficult to retell off. Perhaps control was easier owing to very little rifle-fire from our side and the majority of enemy shells landing on the supports. There was no question of men taking insufficient cover; they melted into the sand after five minutes with an entrenching tool, and during the actual advance they instinctively took advantage of every depression. Officers had no wish to stand up and direct; signallers lay flat with telephones. Stretcher-bearers did not attempt to work in front of the wall. Lewis-gunners suffered; they carried gun and ammunition on the march (there were no mules), and the men were tired; their rushes were not so fast as the platoon advances.

To G.A., lying waiting, before he was hit, came up his sergeant and said, 'That's Mr. Hall over there, sir. I can see him lying dead.'

But G.A. had thoughts which pressed out even grief for his dead friend. 'I shall find time, Cassius, I shall find time.'

Shakespeare might have added these men to those Time stood still withal. For over four hours they lay, within three hundred yards of their invisible foe, under the sleet of bullets. McInerney told me afterwards that it was the heaviest rifle-fire he had known, except the Wadi.[13] The Wadi was the one which made the deepest impression of horror, of all those dreadful and useless slaughters in Aylmer's and Gorringe's attempt to relieve Kut—made this impression, that is, so far as (to paraphrase Macaulay) there is a more or less in extreme horror. And McInerney had seen the 1915 fighting in Flanders. Fortunately the enemy kept most of his shells for farther back. We got plenty in the ruins. But by far the greatest number went far back, where he supposed our reinforcements were coming up. All afternoon we worked in the aid-post under a roof of shells, screaming in both directions, from the enemy and from our own guns. In front the enemy watched the ground so closely that G.A. got his

---

[13] Action of January 13, 1916.

wound by the accident of raising his elbow. But now, as it drew towards noon, there was a clatter as of old iron behind him, and Service, the machine-gunner, rushed up and erected his tripod and lethal toy. No man was more popular than Service in normal times. But to-day he and all his tribe stirred the bitter enmity that Ian Hay tells us the trench-mortar people aroused in France. 'Go away, Service,' his friends entreated. But Service stayed, a fact which precipitated G.A.'s next short rush forward.

On the left the three Indian battalions did a holding attack, pushing out from the wall. They lost heavily. The 53rd Sikhs lost their Colonel (Grattan), their second-in-command (Adams), their adjutant (Blewitt), their quartermaster (Scarth), all killed or died of wounds. The last-named, a very gallant and lovable boy, died in my own aid-post, which he reached after nightfall. On the right Graham, of the machine-gunners, won the V.C. For this battle he was attached to the 56th Rifles. In the advance from the mounds and the heavy fighting on the left all his men became casualties. His gun was knocked out, and he was wounded. McKay, his second-in-command, was hit in the throat, and died. Graham then went back for his other gun. This also was knocked out. Meantime he had collected two more wounds. Compelled to retire, he disabled his second gun completely; then he carried on with the Lewis-gun, though very short of ammunition, till a fourth wound put him out of action. Single-handed he held up a strong counter-attack from the Turks massing on our left. Had these got round, the Leicestershires would have been cut off. It is satisfactory to be able to say that he survived, with no worse hurt than a scar across his face.

Before noon Wilson asked me to take charge of the aid-post. Dobson remained with me; Wilson and Whitehead went up to the wall and established a new A.P. With me were left many stretcher-cases. In the confused character of the ground my place quickly developed into an independent aid-post, and, in addition to receiving a stream of walking cases, methodically passed down by Wilson, had some hundred and thirty wounded, including Turks, who had no other treatment than such as Dobson and I knew how to give. I had never bandaged a man before, but my hands grew red to the elbow. Dobson worked grandly. As far as possible I left our own men to him, and dressed wounded Turks, of whom seventy were sent in late in the afternoon. This was on the *fiat experimentum in corpore vili* principle, as my fingers were unskilled, and yet the work was very great.

About noon a gun was heard on the left bank of the river. Shrapnel burst 'unpleasantly close,' says Hasted, 'to our front line. More followed, and, after bracketing, seemed to centre about two hundred and fifty yards in front of us. We then realized that General Marshall's Column had joined in, supporting us with enfilade gunfire; we were unable to see their target, and could see nothing of the enemy trenches. We could make out single occasional shivering figures moving laterally in the mirage. One Turk was seen throwing up earth, standing up now and then to put up his hands to us. We tried him at ranges of three hundred to twelve hundred yards, but did not even frighten him; observation was absurdly difficult. Firing slackened down, but on the left, out of sight in a depression, we could hear the 56th engaged.'

As Hasted remarks, it seems incredible that our men lay from 11 a.m. till 3.30 p.m. within three hundred yards of the enemy's trenches. Yet such is the fact.

At 4 p.m. we put down a concentrated bombardment of twenty minutes. The Leicestershires, a forlorn and depleted hope, moved swiftly up to within assaulting distance, C Company in reserve behind the right. The 51st Sikhs supported the attack. The 56th Rifles put down the heaviest fire they could, of rifles and all the efficient machine-guns with the Brigade. At 4.20 the guns lifted one hundred yards, and the Leicestershires rushed in. Hasted, watchful behind with C Company, pushed up rapidly to assist the front line. A long line of Turks rose from the ground. All these, and the enemy's second line also, were taken prisoners. Dug-outs were cleared, and many officers were taken, where lofty cliffs overhang the Tigris. These prisoners were sent back with ridiculously weak escorts. They were dazed, their spirits broken. G.A., wounded and falling back in search of the aid-post, came on a large body, wandering sheep without a shepherd. These he annexed, and his orderly led them; he himself, using the famous stick as a crook, coaxed them forward. Prisoners came, ten and twenty in charge of one man. When night had fallen, they sat round us and curiously watched us. Altogether the 'Tigers'—hardly two hundred strong by now—took over eight hundred prisoners. Many of these escaped by reason of the poverty of escort.

But I will not speak of prisoners now. Whilst our scanty stock of ammunition was being fired at the Turks, retiring rapidly, the Leicestershires were pushing far out of reach of telephone communication. 'Limited objectives were not known in the open fighting.'[14] To Captain Diggins fell an amazing success. Suddenly there were flashes almost in his face. 'Guns,' he shouted, and rushed forward. On and on he rushed, till he reached the enemy's guns, he and three of the men of A Company, which he commanded. These guns were in *nullas* by the river-bank. Their crews

---

[14] Hasted.

were sitting round them. Diggins beckoned to them to surrender, which they did. He was so blown with running that he felt sick and faint. Nevertheless he recovered, and rose to the occasion. To us, away in the aid-posts, came epic stories of 'Digguens,' with the ease and magnificence of Sir Francis Drake receiving an admiral's sword, shaking hands with the battery commander. He is a singularly great man in action, is Fred Diggins. In all, from several positions, Diggins took seven fourteen-pounders and two 5.9's. They were badly hit, some of them. The horses were in a wretched condition, none of them unwounded. Several were shot by us almost immediately. Diggins sent his prisoners back, battery commanders and all, in charge of Corporal Williamson and one private. On his way back, after delivering up his prisoners, Williamson was killed.

Very soon on Diggins's arrival his subalterns, Thorpe and McInerney, joined him. He sent them racing back across the perilous mile which now lay between them and the wall. Thorpe went to Lieutenant-Colonel Knatchbull, and McInerney to Creagh, the second-in-command this day. All did their best to get reinforcements. The two other brigades, however badly hit the previous day, were now close up. The 19th Brigade, becoming aware of the situation, eagerly put their services at our disposal. After the action the official explanation of the loss of the guns was that the Leicestershires got out of hand and went too far; so I was told in the colloquial language which I have set down. A nearer explanation is that they went because of over-confidence somewhere back. Night was falling, and the guns already gone, when reinforcements from the 19th Brigade came past my aid-post and asked me the direction. Had the guns been kept, I verily believe at least one V.C. would have come our way, for Diggins, and M.C.'s for his lieutenants. As it was, Diggins got an M.C. and Thorpe a 'mention.' Nothing came to McInerney, who was one of the many soldiers who went through years of battle, always doing their duty superbly, but emerging ribbonless at the end. Six months later, at Tekrit, these guns took a heavy toll from our infantry. Now, after all effort, scarcely fifty men could be got up to them.

In these exalted moments of victory, glorious almost beyond belief, Sergeant-Major Whatsize fell, twenty yards from the enemy's line. In his last minutes he was happy, as a child is happy.

The handful at the guns waited. A large barrel of water had been put there for the Turkish gunners. This was drained to the last drop. The guns were curiously examined. 'Besides the intricate mechanism and beautifully finished gear, there were some German sextants and range-finders, compasses like those on a ship's binnacle, and other instruments on a lavish scale,' says Hasted. But this inspection was cut short, for now came the counter-attack. The Turks began to shell the captured gun-position. Then, from the railway-embankment, nearly a mile to the Leicestershires' left front, several lines of Turks emerged, in extended formation, a distance of fifty yards between each line. At least two thousand were heading for the fifty Leicestershires holding the guns. 'It was like a crowd at a football-match,' a spectator told me.

Diggins sent word to Lowther, commanding B Company, a little to his left rear, 'The Turks are counter-attacking.' Lowther replied that he was falling back. Diggins and Hasted fell back in conformity. Hasted was asking his men how many rounds of ammunition they had left. None had more than five rounds, so perforce we ceased fire. The 51st Sikhs, with the exception of Subahdar Aryan Singh and two sepoys, had not appeared. The Leicestershires damaged the guns as they might for half a dozen fevered, not to say crowded, minutes of glorious life. Hasted, who was one of those who enjoyed this destruction, complains that they did not know much about what to do; they burred the breech-block threads and smashed the sights with pick-axes. The Mills bombs put in the bores did not explode satisfactorily. Then they fell back. One of the sergeants was hit in the chest, Sergeant Tivey, a Canadian; he was put on one of the Turkish *garrons* and led along. 'From the attention he received from the enemy's guns, they must have thought him a Field-Marshal.'[15] The Turks, for all their force, crept up timidly. After securing the guns, they raced to Tekrit, thirty miles away. But they sent a large body in pursuit of the retreating 'Tigers.'

The Leicestershires fell back rapidly, the enemy pressing hard. The 51st Sikhs were found, hidden by the hollows of the ground; they had been a buttress to the left flank of that handful of adventurous infantry in their forward sweep into the heart of the Turkish position. It was now that Graham and the 56th Rifles checked the counter-attack, which threatened to drive a wedge between the Leicestershires and the river. The whole front was now connected up, and, in face of an attacking army, British and Indians dug themselves in. The 51st sent along some ammunition. The sun was setting, and in the falling light the last scene of this hard-fought day took place. Turkish officers could be seen beating their men with the flat of their swords. The enemy came, rushing and halting. The sun, being behind them, threw a clear field of observation before them; but over them it flung a glamour and dimness, in which they moved, a shadow-army, silhouettes that

---

[15] Hasted.

made a difficult mark. And our men were down to their last rounds of ammunition. Our guns opened again, but too late, and did not find their target. But the Leicestershires' bombers, sixty men in all, were thrown forward, bringing ammunition which saved the day. Thirty of the sixty fell in that rush. The Turks were now within two hundred and fifty yards; but here they wavered. For half an hour they kept up a heavy rifle-fire. Then, at six o'clock, the 19th Brigade poured in, and the thin lines filled up with Gurkhas, Punjabis, and Seaforths. Moreover, the new-comers had abundance of ammunition. Darkness fell, and our line pushed forward. For over two hours we could hear the Turks man-handling their guns away. But there were strong covering-parties, and our patrols were driven back with loss. Our guns put down a spasmodic and ineffectual fire. Then all became quiet. All along the enemy's line of retreat and far up the river were flares and bonfires. Away in Samarra buildings were in flames, and down the Tigris floated two burning barges, of which more hereafter.

I cannot speak as they deserve of the gallant work of the Indian regiments. The severity of their losses is eloquent testimony. 'Boomer' Barrett came down the field, shot through the face, cheerfully announcing his good luck: 'I've got a soft one, right through the cheek.'

I have spoken of the 53rd Sikhs. They lost their four senior officers, killed. But every regiment had brave leaders to mourn. One thinks with grief and admiration of that commander, a noble and greatly beloved man, whom a bullet struck down, so that he died without recovering consciousness several days later. Though the body's tasks were finished, his mind worked on the fact that his men had been temporarily checked, and he kept up the cry, 'What will they say in England? The —— fell back; ——

failed them.' Even so, when duty has become life's ruling atmosphere,

> *One stern tyrannic thought which makes*
> *All other thoughts its slave,*

it matters little that the body should fail. The mind labours yet, fulfilling its unconscious allegiance.

> *He went, unterrified,*
> *Into the Gulf of Death.*

In my aid-post we carried on, secure beneath our canopy of racing shells. The slope gave cover against 'over' bullets, except when it was necessary to walk about. Early in the afternoon, during a lull, a doctor appeared and asked if it was safe to bring up his ambulances. I told him 'Yes'; there were dropping bullets, but very little shell-fire. He replied that he would come immediately. But the supply of shells greatly quickened, and he did not appear again till near darkness, when he brought two motor ambulances, taking five sitting and four lying cases in each. He promised to return, but did not. Apart from these eighteen, only the walking wounded got away, pushing back into our noisy and perilous hinterland.

About four o'clock the Turks, in reply to our intense bombardment, put a brief but terrific fire on the mounds, blowing up men on every side. I decided to clear out to where, round the corner, an old wall gave upright shelter. As our first exodus swung round, a huddled, hobbling mass, two 'coal-boxes' burst in quick succession, each closer than the last shell before it. I shouted 'Duck!' We ducked, then made a few yards and ducked for the second time. A perfect sleet of wind and steel seemed to pass overhead. But no one was hit, and we were round the corner, where, I fear, I dropped the Cherub with considerable emphasis on his gammy leg. But indeed we were very lucky. Shells burst on every side of the aid-post—on right and left, but not on us. This was one of the rare occasions when I have felt confidence. Dobson and I were far too busied to worry. Also it seemed hard to believe that a shell would be allowed to fall on that shattered, helpless suffering. I saw, without seeing, things that are burnt into memory. We had no *morphia*, nothing but bandages. There was a man hit in the head, who just flopped up and down, seemingly invertebrate as an eel, calling out terribly for an hour till he died. Another man, also hit in the head—but he recovered, and I afterwards met him in Bombay—kept muttering, 'Oh those guns! They go through my head!'

A large body of prisoners was massed in the hollow beside us. When these marched off, some seventy wounded were sent to me, under the impression that the place was a regular aid-post. They were horribly smashed. General Thomson's Brigade (14th Division) had enfiladed them with artillery fire from the other bank, with dreadful effect. He got into their reserves, their retreat, their hospitals, and broke them up. In one place his fire caught a body of Turks massing for a counter-attack, beneath big bluffs by the water, and heaped the sand with dead and maimed. These men came with their gaping wounds and snapped limbs. Private Clifton, a friend of mine, brought bucket after bucket of water from the river. They drank almost savagely. My inexpert fingers hurt cruelly as I bandaged them, and they winced and cried. But the next minute they would stroke my hand, to show they understood good intentions. They had a great belief in the superiority of our civilization—at any rate in its medical aspect. They insisted, those who had been bandaged by the Turkish aid-posts, in tearing off their bandages—perfectly good ones, but smaller than ours—and on having new bandages from me. Just when the 5.9's blew us round the corner, Waller, adjutant of the 56th Brigade, R.F.A., came up and asked if I could send any one to look at some men just hit by the tornado. Mester Dobson was as busied as a man could be, his inevitable pipe in his mouth, so I went with Waller. One man was breathing, his head broken behind; the others were dead. Beside one of the corpses was a red mass. I saw, noting the fact automatically and without the least squeamishness, that it was his brains. We carried the living man in.

In the darkness Dobson came and said. 'There's a wounded officer just come in. I've given him a drink and dressed him.' A minute later he said, 'That officer's dead, sir.' I went across, and found it was Scarth, of the 53rd. No braver spirit went out in this day of storm and sorrow than this very gallant boy. He was aged nineteen.

> *Night fell, and slowly o'er the blood-bought mile*
> *They brought a broken body, frail but brave;*
> *A boy who carried into death the smile*
> *With which he thanked for water that we gave.*
> *Steadfast among the steadfast, those who kept*
> *The narrow pass whereby the Leicesters swept,*
> *Amid the mounded sands of ancient pride*
> *He sleeps where Grattan fell and Adams died.*

I know his father, and the Himalayan oaks and pines amid which he grew to manhood. Men looking on Scarth loved him. The freshness of his mountain home and his free, happy life clung to him to this end, amid the tumults and terrors of our desert battle.

> *The son of Hyrtacus, whom Ide*
> *Sent, with his quiver at his side,*

*From hunting beasts in forest-brake,*
*To follow in Æneas' wake.*[16]

At dusk Wilson came. He had been toiling away, exposed and close up to the fighters, as always—there never was a braver regimental medical officer—and he now asked me to be responsible for getting his wounded away, whilst he searched the battlefield. So all his cases were evacuated into my place. At the same time many chits reached me, addressed to the O.C. Clearing-Station. As there was no such person, I opened these. The regimental aid-posts were pressing to be cleared. My own place had men from seven different regiments, British and Indian, as well as Turks, and Wilson was sending more along. So I found McLeod, and we 'phoned down to the field ambulances. These were congested from yesterday's battle and to-day's walking cases, and replied that nothing could be done till dawn. But we were so insistent that about midnight bullock-carts turned up, and I got fifty wounded away. The *cahars*,[17] in their zeal to remove all kit belonging to the wounded, carried off my water-bottle, haversack, rations, and communion-kit. But before this I had been down to the Tigris in the darkness, and drunk like a wounded wolf.

To return to the battle as it died away. The Forward Observing Officer with the Leicestershires sent word back that fourteen guns (instead of nine) had been taken. The news was exultantly forwarded to Corps H.Q. When the case proved to be nine only, and those nine lost again, the message was allowed to stand, the authorities hoping against hope that the guns would walk back into our possession. And Fortune was very good to them. Those guns,

---

[16] Æneid, Book IX, Conington's translation.
[17] Indian hospital orderlies and bearers.

indeed, came not back; but, as darkness fell, two burning barges, as already mentioned, floated down the river. One was exploding, like a magazine on fire. This contained ammunition. The other barge, when pulled to shore, was found to contain fourteen field-guns, the number specified to Corps—old guns, but serviceable. Johnny, despairing of getting these away, had set fire to the barge to sink them. So the original message stood, and our loss could be glossed over. And the wastefulness of sinking quite good guns was avoided.

The night was sleepless, bitterly cold. Dobson and I kept a watch for Arabs. I sat beside a dead man, and shared his oil-sheet. A few more wounded came in after midnight, among them Sergeant Tivey. All night long wounded Turks crawled the battlefields and cried in the cold. But I heard none of them, for there were groans much nearer. Our unwounded prisoners were crowded into a *nulla*. Among them was the Turkish Artillery Brigade Commander, who knew some English and kept insisting on a hearing from time to time. But all he ever said was, 'Yes, gentlemen, you have got my guns, but, what is far worse, you have got me.' Had we cared, we might have cheered him with the information that we had not got his guns, but only himself. Yet, considering the relative value, in his eyes, of himself and these, such information would hardly have consoled him.

In this battle occurred a case of a man being 'fey.' An officer gave his kit and money to his batman, for distribution to his platoon, the previous night. As he went into action a friend exchanged greetings. He replied, 'Yes, but I'm afraid I'm not coming back to-day.' No one saw him fall, but he was found dead in the mounds, with several wounds.

The east was reddening when I saw Haughton, Staff-

Captain of the 19th Brigade, on the hillock above the aid-post. This Brigade H.Q. were my best friends in the division. I begged a mug of tea from him, so we went along together. I found General Peebles and Brigade-Major Thornhill, and they gave me an excellent breakfast.

The 28th Brigade moved on, following the 21st Brigade, who occupied Samarra. But the wounded remained. Shortly after dawn the medical folk, in fulfilment of their promise, sent up an ordinary motor-car and took away two sitting cases. Nothing else happened. Time passed, and the heat was getting up. So I wandered back some miles, and found hospital-tents. Here was Father Bernard Farrell, the Roman Catholic padre, slaving, as he had done all night. I saw Westlake, and Sowter, who was dying. 'It's been a great fight, padre,' said Sowter, 'a great fight. I'm getting better.' No loss was felt more severely than that of this quiet, able man. He had seen much fighting in France, and in this, his first action with us, he impressed every one with his coolness and efficiency. He had walked across to Lowther, his company commander, to draw his attention to a new and threatening movement of the enemy. Then, as he stopped to bandage a wounded sergeant, a bullet pierced his stomach. The same bullet, leaving his body, went through both legs of Sergeant Lang, the one bullet making six holes. Sowter had been with us one week. I never knew any one whose influence went so deep in so brief a time.

> *Our seven-days' guest, he came and went his ways,*
> *Walking the darkness garlanded with praise!*
> *Our seven-days' guest! Yet love that this man gained*
> *Others have scarce in three-score years attained.*

The hospital-tents were congested with wounded, and the responsible officer declined to take any more. They had no more stretchers, all being used as beds, and no more space. Fortunately an order came from Division that they must immediately remove some wounded Turks.

I said, 'I have some wounded Turks.'

'Yes, but I'm afraid those aren't the Turks meant.'

'Well,' I replied, 'I've been up all night, and I'm very footsore. You might at least give me a lift back.'

This was conceded, and I returned in the first of five motor-ambulances. The corporal-in-charge had no idea where he was to find the wounded Turks, so I swept him into my place. This I cleared of everyone but a few horribly wounded prisoners, and sent on a note to the M.O. of the 51st Sikhs.

The previous day two wounded Turks, a machine-gun officer and a Red Crescent orderly, had arrived in the aid-post. The latter helped nobly with the wounded, so I had a note sent down with them, that they had earned good treatment. The officer had a friend from the same military college in Stamboul, which friend had a ghastly shell-wound in his back. What happened, I think, was this. When his friend was knocked out, the unwounded officer—they were both boys, well under twenty—brought up a medical orderly. All three were then overwhelmed by our rush, and in the confusion the unwounded men kept with the other, to see that he got treatment when opportunity came. So they slipped into my aid-post, where they stopped all night, making no offer to escape.

I sent a message to Brigade, but their reply, a verbal one which did not reach me till next evening, was that they had better stay where they were. The unwounded officer's silent anxiety for his friend was most touching, and I pushed the latter away with the midnight convoy.

Next morning I sent both officer and orderly to the nearest prisoners' camp; but the sergeant-in-charge returned them, with word that he took only wounded prisoners. So I had to keep them. Weir, the staff-captain, joined me, and we talked to the officer in French while we waited for the divisional second line to come up. We were puzzled as to why the Turks left a position so strong as Istabulat before being actually driven out.

The officer's reply was, 'Because of the *tiar*' (aeroplane).

I cannot follow this, unless, misunderstanding us, he was referring to this second day's fight and the aeroplane brought down at the beginning. Perhaps, being afraid to send up any other 'planes, they were deceived as to our number. He insisted that we had had three divisions in action, and was mortified when we told him the truth.

The sun was getting very hot, and, since no more ambulances came, we were troubled for the few pitifully smashed Turks who still remained. We got covers of sorts for them, though we could not prevent the flies from festooning their wounds. 'It's up to us to do our best,' said Weir. 'We shouldn't care for it if our wounded were left by them.' In the afternoon ambulances began to arrive, and I evacuated these few and saw the evacuation of the Indian regimental A.P.'s commence. My dead were buried, and their graves effaced, so far as possible, against prowling Buddus. The second line arrived, so my prisoners and I set out on our tired trudge to Samarra.

I told the Turks of our Somme successes (as we then took them to be) and our more recent March victories in Flanders, pointing out the big improvement.

'In the beginning we had little artillery, but now we have much.'

'Beaucoup,' he repeated, with conviction. In every way one spared a brave enemy's feelings. Last year they had won; now it was our turn. 'That is so,' said he.

This thought comforted him, and the memory of their great triumphs before Kut in early 1916. Did he not wear a medal for those days? *'Pour le mérite,'* the orderly proudly told me. I begged scraps of biscuits from men on the march, and we shared them. I expressed regret for this march on empty stomachs.

*'C'est toujours la marche,'* said the officer, shrugging his shoulders.

Truly, it must have been; a nightmare of rapid movement and sleeplessness even for us who pursued—hammer and chase ever since Maude broke up the Turkish lines before Kut. As we marched I found that the Indians took us for three prisoners and not two, I being a German officer. But when J.Y. cantered up and hailed me, a laugh ran down the column, with the words 'Padre Sahib.' At Samarra the first person we ran into was General Peebles, to whom I handed over my prisoners, with a request that they should be fed. Haughton promised to see to this. Then a pleasant thing happened. The Turkish officer stepped quickly up to me, saluted, and held out his hand. I saluted back, and we shook hands. They were good fellows, both officer and orderly, and carried themselves like free men.

It was now 5 p.m. I joined the 'Tigers.' Fowke and Lowther had each killed a snake after laying their blankets down. They gave me good greeting. I fed and washed, then slept abundantly.

For the two Istabulat battles the official return of captures was: Twenty officers and six hundred and sixty-seven men, one 5.9, fourteen Krupp field-guns, two machine-guns, twelve hundred and forty rifles, a quantity of hand-grenades, two hundred rounds of gun-ammunition, five hundred and forty thousand rounds of rifle-ammunition, four limbers, sixteen engines, two hundred and forty trucks, one crane, spare wheels and other stores, two munitions barges. Samarra Station was dismantled, but the engines and trucks were there. Up to the last the Turk had meant to keep the railhead, so the engines were only partly disabled, boilers having been removed from some and other parts from others. By putting parts of engines together we got a sufficiency of usable engines. Within a fortnight we had trains running.

For the battle of the 22nd both Diggins and Lowther got M.C.'s. If it was the former's élan which carried our wave into the enemy's guns, the latter's judgement played a great part in extricating us without disaster. Hasted, the alert and watchful, had already been gazetted after the fall of Baghdad as D.S.O. He left us shortly after, returning to his own regiment, the Durham Light Infantry, in India. In Rawal Pindi he delivered a lecture on the action in which he had played so brilliant a part.

It would be interesting to know if Hasted has ever had an enemy. His personal charm is almost greater than any man has a right to have, especially when the Gods have already made that man an able soldier and administrator. But it is an unfair world.

These awards were announced in a Gazette nearly a year later. To Sowter, had he lived, would have fallen a third M.C. Fowke, as well as Thorpe, got a 'mention,' of which he was utterly unaware, being away sick, till I ran into him in Kantara[18] in 1918, about eleven o'clock at night. I roused him from sleep for a chat. When I told him of his 'mention,' he considered that I was making a very successful attempt to be humorous, and laughed himself to sleep again. At intervals till dawn I heard him still laughing in his dreams at a notion so ridiculous.

---

[18] On the Suez Canal.

I hope that some other will tell of the deeds of the Indian regiments. Even more I hope that some one will tell, as I cannot, of the gallant and costly charge which our cavalry made on the Turkish trenches to our left, a charge which staggered the enemy as he swung round to cut off the Leicestershires. The 32nd Lancers lost, among others, their Colonel (Griffiths) and their Adjutant (Captain Hunter), killed.

These two days' fighting at Istabulat and for Samarra cost us about two thousand four hundred casualties. The 28th Brigade, on the 22nd, lost four hundred and forty-six men. The enemy's losses, including prisoners, must have been at least three thousand.

My one note for April 24 is 'Flies.' It was high summer, and in the terrible and waxing heats we lay for over a month longer, with no tents, and with no shelter save our blanket-bivvies. We were the more wretched in that we occupied an old enemy camp, and were entered into full possession of its legacy of filth and flies. On the first Sunday my morning service was swathed in dust, one swirling misery, and I was sore tempted to preach, foreseeing the days to come, on *'These are but the beginning of sorrows.'*

CHAPTER 5

# Summer and Waiting

Samarra was entered on April 23, the 21st and 8th Brigades going through the 19th and 28th Brigades. These brigades followed during the course of the day, and the ridge of Al-Ajik fell into our hands. From Samarra northwards high bluffs run with the river, pushing out to it from plateaus stretching across the heart of Jezireh and climbing again beyond the river to the Jebel Hamrin. Below the bluffs are wide spaces of dead ground, beds which the Tigris has forsaken. On the right bank, before the dead ground begins and directly opposite Samarra town, is a plain some ten or dozen miles in length, between the mounds of the battle of April 22 and the crest of Al-Ajik; this plain may be three miles broad. Al-Ajik covers and commands all approaches from the north, and, with the central plateau, shuts the plain within a crescent. Here, behind Al-Ajik, lay our camp for the next seven months.

North from Al-Ajik the plateau rolls away to Tekrit, and the same rolling country lies to westward also, broken with *nulla* and water-hole. To Tekrit, more than twenty miles beyond, the Turkish Army fled.

Samarra is a dirty, sand-coloured town, with no touch of brightness but what its famous dome gives it. This dome it was that shone over against the sunset, the last earthly beauty for so many eyes, on that evening of savage battle when the 7th Division flung out its leading brigade and reached, all but held, the Turkish guns. The dome hides the cavern into which the Twelfth Imam vanished, and from which he will emerge, bringing righteousness to a faithless world. Just beyond the dome rises the corkscrew tower, built in imitation of the Babylonian ziggurats. To the north-east is 'Julian's Tomb,' a high pyramid in the desert. It was near Samarra that he suffered defeat and died of wounds. For twenty miles round, in Beit Khalifa, Eski Baghdad, and elsewhere, is one confused huddle of ruins. It is hard to believe that such tawdry magnificence as Harun's successors intermittently brought to the town during the precarious times of Abbasid decay is responsible for all these arches and caverns and tumbled bricks. Major Kenneth Mason, already mentioned as having identified Xenophon's Sittake, has collected good reasons for placing Opis, once the great mart of the East, at Eski Baghdad, and not where the maps conjecturally place it, twenty miles farther down Tigris. In summer, green is none save in patches by the river; but a thin scurf of yellow grass and coarse herbage overspread the ruins, in which were abundant partridges and quails. Germans had been excavating before we came, and we found in the town many cases of antiquities, ready packed for transport to Europe. The 7th Division, digging their positions, presently found pottery, glazed fragments, and tear-bottles.

The town is walled, and sits above steep bluffs. Tigris, swift and clear like a mountain stream, races by, dividing round an island. Below the town is another island, with an expanse of shingle towards the right bank; to this island Divisional Head Quarters went, a most unfair avoidance of the 'dust-devils' which plagued their brethren. Here were tamarisk thickets, haunted with great metallic beetles, with such wings as Eastern smiths know how to use. The green bushes were good to the eyes, and a pleasant curtain from flying sand. But a sudden rise in the river flushed its shallow right arm, and made the place an island in reality and all inconvenience. The righteous, seeing this, rejoiced.

The brigades scattered over the plain, the 8th Brigade going on, after brief pause, to the ravines and jungles of the Adhaim, where the war was dying. May's first week swept the Turk out of the Adhaim Valley, and our troops settled down for the summer.

The brigades scattered; blankets came up, and we slept. For over a month we had only bivvies, the usual rifle-supported blanket, tugging and straining at the stones which held it whenever a 'dust-devil' danced by or a sandstorm arose. But E.P.[19] tents dribbled in. Even mails began to arrive, and parcels; and to me, on the first day of ease, came a jubilant telegram from my old friends of the 19th Brigade: 'Come and have tea with us. We have a cake!' I went, and found them where the shingles led to Divisional Island. Blue rollers swung themselves on the air below the cliffs; and on the pebbles an owl skipped and danced, showing off in the beautiful evening sunlight. This was a daily performance, Thornhill told me. It had been General Peebles' birthday, and the brag about the cake was splendidly justified. There were buns also.

Summer dragged by. In Baghdad pomegranates blossomed, mulberries fruited, figs ripened. But in Samarra the desert throbbed and shimmered in the growing and great heats. Worst of all, we missed the dates. The fresh dates are the one solace of Mesopotamia. My campaigning

---

[19] European privates'.

recollections are embittered by this memory, that both my two date-seasons were spent up the line, at Sannaiyat and Samarra, where dates never came. Till mid-May the nights remained cool. Mesopotamia's extremes are amazing. After a day intolerable as I have found very few days in India will come a night, not close and sleepless as an Indian night, but cool, even cold. In the April fighting we found the nights bitter. So May gave us a fortnight of tolerable nights; but then fire settled on the land. The flies all died. But the infantry had an elaborate trench-system to dig, so they were not able to die. The ground was solid gypsum.

Changes happened. Generals Peebles and Davies went to India on leave. The enemy's Intelligence Department, alert as ever, noted the fact, and gave it out that our losses in the Istabulat battles were even heavier than they had supposed at first, for two generals had left the front, casualties. Such a statement was twice blessed: it cheered the enemy, and cheered us also. In my own brigade Thorpe became staff-captain, in place of Weir, who went home. To all the Leicestershires, and to me especially, Thorpe's going was a heavy loss. 'I could have better spared a better man.' I must henceforth botanize alone. No longer could he teach young subalterns to 'practise music'—in the Socratic sense, that the best music was philosophy—to be repaid with their affectionate regard as 'Daddy.' He wrote to me, a month after his going, that he was becoming as 'great a horseman as John Wesley'; and he lost weight during that summer. He lost a good deal his first week, and in this manner. The Bishop of Nagpur was due to visit us, and all who had subscribed their religion officially as 'C. of E.' were commanded to brighten belts and buttons for a service parade on Wednesday at 6 ak. emma. The parade was held, every one arriving, of course, considerably before the hour. The Divisional General was there, and many generals and colonels; in fact, every Anglican of note, except Thorpe, who sent word, about 6.30, that he had made a mistake, and the service was to be next day, Thursday, at the same hour. At this announcement a wave of uncontrollable grief swept over the vast assembly, and for some days Thorpe was a fugitive. But he returned to normal courses, and in time even this witty inauguration of his reign was forgiven. But I had many inquiries as to the tenets of Wesleyanism.

For me, I went sick; recovered; and went sick again, drifting down-stream, and to India. But first Thornhill, Bracken the machine-gunner, and I explored Al-Ajik.

Once upon a time the river had washed the foot of Al-Ajik ridge. But now a long stretch of dead ground intervenes before water is reached. Local legend says a lady lived here who played Hero to a Leander on the opposite bank. More obviously, Al-Ajik castle guarded Samarra from the north. The castle is on steep crags, with vast *nullas* in front. In the old days it should have been impregnable. Underneath are very large vaults, filled with rubbish. As our exploring party came up a pair of hawks left their eyrie, and circled round us, screaming their indignation. When the division first reached Al-Ajik, Thornhill said, a pair of Egyptian vultures (Pharaoh's Chickens) were nesting here. These had gone. They are rare birds in Mesopotamia, and I never saw them north of Sheikh Saad. Thornhill had seen Brahminy Duck in a *nulla*, so we searched till we found a tunnel. Bracken leading, we got in some hundred yards, stooping and striking matches, till we came on a heap of bones. Thornhill surmised a hyena, so we returned, as no one wished to fight even that, unarmed and in a diameter of less than five feet. There must be many tunnels leading into the heart of Al-Ajik fortress; and here, as everywhere on the plateau, were remains of the most complicated irrigation system the ancient world knew. The castle, as it stands, has been largely built out of the ruined portions on its northern face.

Life was scant at Samarra, as poor as it had been abundant at Sannaiyat. The crested larks were of a new species. Owls nested in the old wells; and most units were presently owning their owlets or kestrels or speckled kingfishers, miserable-looking birds. Sand grouse were few, but commoner towards the central plateau, where were water-holes. Gazelles were often seen by pickets, and used to break across the railway-line, to water at the river. One regiment took a Lewis-gun after them, and other folk chased them in motor-cars. The British army, as ever, busied itself, as opportunity came, in its self-appointed task of simplifying the country's fauna that the naturalist's work might be easier. Wherefore the gazelles left our precincts, but still haunted the channels of the Dujail, by Beled and Istabulat. For most of the year the water-holes sufficed them, the green, velvet dips, with *zizyph*-bushes fringing each hollow, which redeem the desert. Hedgehog quills and skins were common, as everywhere in Mesopotamia. A vast hedgehog led C Company of the Leicestershires nightly to their picket-stations. On its first appearance a man ran to bayonet it, but the officer did not see the necessity of this, and stopped him. So the urchin lived, and ever after paced gravely before its friends. Then we had the usual birds. Storks nested in the town; there were rollers and kingfishers, and a hawk or two. But the desert, with its starved crop of dwarf thorns, had no place for bird or animal. Men who saw Samarra after my time raved of its winter glory, its irises, its grass knee-high, its splendid anemones. But in summer the land lay desolate. Nothing abounded but scorpions, *mantidae*, and grasshoppers.

And nothing happened but the heat. In July, in ghastly heat, men were expected to take Ramadie. They failed, most of their heavy casualties being from heat-stroke. But that was the Connaught Rangers and a Euphrates affair. At Samarra we experienced nothing more dangerous than Fritz's[20] visits. Once or twice he bombed the station. When the railway began running, there were two accidental derailments, in the second of which several men were killed and General Maude had a narrow escape. By Sumaikchah a British officer and his Indian escort were waylaid and murdered. The murderers were outlawed; but a year later the first on our list of the whole gang walked back into occupied territory and was taken and hanged, despite the wish of the Politicals to spare him. Of all these events, such as they were, we heard from Barron—'the bold, bad Barron,' who left the Leicestershires to take up 'important railway duties' pending the renewal of fighting.

These matters are dull enough; but no recital can be so dull as the times were, and we had to live through them. At Samarra the division worked unmolested through the awful heats, digging the hard ground, cutting avenues for machine-gun fire, making strong points. Wilson had gone, but he had an adequate successor in Haigh. Thanks to him, the Leicestershires established the singular fact that Samarra is the healthiest spot in the world. One man died, in place of the dreadful sequence of deaths a year before at Sannaiyat. The division's daily sick-rate was .9 a thousand! The Leicestershires and the Indian battalions did even better. And yet we spent the summer in a place where fresh

---

[20] A new Fritz, of course. The old one was killed at Istabulat.

vegetables were unprocurable, except a most inadequate supply of melons and (rarely) beans. Djinns scoured the plain, and at any hour of any day half a score of 'dust-devils' could be seen racing or sweeping majestically along—each *djinn* seemed to make his own wind and choose his own pace—now towering to a height of several hundred feet, with vast, swirling base, and now trailing a tenuous mist across a *nulla*. Our few hens ran panting into the tents, ejected at one door, only to enter at another. And yet, as I have said, only one man died—with the battalion, that is—and ridiculously few went sick. But by Colonel Knatchbull's death in Baghdad the battalion lost its commander, and the division a very fine soldier. Wounded at Sheikh Saad in January, 1916, he had returned in time for the three railhead battles. He struggled on with sickness, refusing to contemplate a second leave to India, and died at midsummer.

The worst of the heats I escaped. After a spell in Beit Na'ama, the delightful estuary-side officers' hospital, a tangle of citron and fig-groves, with vines making cool roofs, and with the Shat-el-Arab flowing by, I was discharged. Feeling more wretched than ever, I lingered on at Busra in the poisonous billets, filthy Arab houses, named by their present occupants 'Flea Villa,' 'Bug Cottage,' 'Muddy View' (this would be for winter; the world nowhere else holds such mud as Busra mud). Busra is hateful beyond words; any place up the line is preferable, except perhaps Twin Canals[21] and Beled. I was to be returned to duty 'in due course'; but the Transport authorities were never in a hurry. It was like being slowly baked in a brick oven. I had spent ten days so, with no prospect of being given a boat

---

[21] Below Kut, on the right bank of the Tigris. A pestilential haunt in 1916.

up-stream, when some one told General Fane, the O.C. 7th Division, that I had been very sick and was waiting to get back to duty. He said, 'Nonsense,' and sent a wire direct to G.H.Q., insisting that I be given a month's leave in India. I got it immediately. But for this action, leave could not have come my way. No division ever had a kinder O.C. than Fane. He knew every one, and was constantly doing thoughtful acts such as this.

India, when it found time to give thought to Mesopotamia, chattered of the tremendous Turco-German offensive which was to sweep down from Mosul in the autumn. When I returned, at the end of August, all down the line I found excitement. Only at Samarra itself was quiet and ease of mind, where old comrades greeted me joyously and introduced new-comers. There was Fergusson, reputed to have half a century of ranching and horse-dealing in the Argentine; 'Forty-nine,' said Fowke, in a delighted whisper, assessing his age. (As a matter of fact, Fergusson's years were forty-one.) There was 'Ezra' ('Likewise Beetle,' interpolated Fowke), who had arrived the day I went sick. 'Ezra,' who signed his name as Mason, and was brother of Kenneth Mason, engineer and archaeologist, got his nickname from a supposed modelling of his bald dome upon Ezra's Tomb, by Q'urna. Keely, classical scholar and philosopher, was standing outside his tent, pondering, as I came up to rejoin the battalion. He called me up, and asked me earnestly what girl from Greek literature I should like to have known, even to have had as companion on the Thames at Richmond. '*Nausicaa*,' I said. 'Every time,' agreed Keely, brightening up as if a heavy load had been lifted from his mind, and begged me to have a drink in her honour. Bale and Charles Copeman were away, by Al-Ajik; 'in the nearest E.P. tent to Constantinople,' G.A.

said. Of our wounded, only G.A. was back. Warren came later; Westlake remained in India.

Some surprise was expressed that I had returned at all. This was Thorpe's doing. To explain, I must go back a little. I knew Thorpe years before the war. We met again in Sannaiyat trenches. His messmates, who desired to know more of Thorpe's old life, asked me how we met first. 'I was chaplain of a jail at Peterborough,' I replied. The statement was received at once; the only head on which further light was sought was as to the number of years that were deducted from his sentence for service in Mesopotamia. (Convicts from India who came out in the Labour Corps to Mesopotamia were remitted ten years.) Now, during my Indian leave, an old friend found me out and took me to spend the last days of my Darjiling visit with him. He was, among other things, superintendent of the prison. I carelessly wrote to Thorpe on a sheet of paper with the printed heading 'Jail-house, Darjiling.' Thorpe spent July and August in taking this sheet round from mess to mess. He blackened my reputation, and opened up a field of speculation as to the reason of my incarceration. 'No doubt this man is a murderer, whom, though he hath escaped from the sea'—from Mesopotamia, say— 'yet Justice hath not suffered to live.' He considered that he was level with me for my Peterborough jail-jape, and was much cheered.

It took the best part of September to get up-stream and back to Samarra. When the boat reached Busra, scores of men were prostrate on the deck from heat-stroke and exhaustion. In the Gulf I had a funeral. I tried to skip to the finish of the service, with the page shimmering and jumping before me, but had to hand the book to the captain as I reeled down. He threw the body over, and every one flew up-deck. Later, on the up-stream trip, we realized the fact on which all Mesopotamia agreed, that for sheer horror the deck of a P-boat[22] is unrivalled. Possibly it is due to the glare from the water, but our daily temperatures of between 115° and 125° in the shade seemed a hundredfold higher than they were. Just below Kut we were held up for several days in a camp; not even Sheikh Saad in the old, bad days was more cursed with sandflies.

I had for companion on board Kenneth Mason, engineer and archaeologist. We passed Sannaiyat and the winding reaches where every earth-scar and mound had a history. Here the Turk had blown up the ammunition barges, and for hundreds of yards inland the ground was still strewn with twisted scrap-iron; here he had set his 5.9's on the balloon, and the evening fishing had been interrupted; here used to be the advanced dressing-station in the times of trench warfare; here was Left Bank Group, where our guns had been, the tamarisk thickets and wheeling harriers, and the old shell-holes on the beach. Those crumbling sandbanks were Mason's Mounds, and those were Crofton's O. Pip.[23] Here were Abu Roman Mounds, and here the lines of Nakhailat or Suwada; here were the Beit Aiessa defences; here those of Abdul Hassan and E Mounds. It was on that angle that the Julnar grounded in that despairing, impossible attempt to run the blockade and bring food to Townshend's men. It was in that scrub that the Turks and H.L.I.[24] crashed when both sides launched a simultaneous attack.

We passed Kut. The river was low, and the people were growing lettuce, while they might, on the dried sandbanks. The town front against the palms showed its shell-

---

[22] Paddle-boat.
[23] Observation post.
[24] Highland Light Infantry.

holes and caverns, and we remembered how we used to see the city, from Dujaileh Redoubt, rising up like a green promontory. From Townshend's first battle there to the day when the 7th Division occupied the lines of Suwada, Kut cost us not less in battle casualties than sixty thousand men. One makes no computation of the dead in the old cholera camps by Abu Roman, or in a score of cemeteries from Sannaiyat and Es-Sinn to Bombay, who perished in that time when

> *the shark-tracked ships went down*
> *To Bombay Town.*

Kut will be a place of pilgrimage, and deserves to be, even among the many shrines of this war. From Sheikh Saad to Shumran is one graveyard and battlefield, a stretch of thirty miles, where over twenty pitched battles took place, many being British defeats. At Kut itself Townshend's old trenches can be traced; and in the town are broken buildings, and, to eastward, the monument erected by the Turks. Across the river is the Shat-el-Hai and its complicated and costly battlefields, and the relics of the famous liquorice factory which Townshend held, and which we took, in 1917, almost last of all. At Shumran, above the town, is the place of the great crossing. And on the ribs of sand, when water is low, are liquorice-stacks and lettuce-beds.

> *The mud-strips green with lettuce, red with stacks*
> *Of liquorice; shattered walls, and gaping caves:*
> *Beyond, the shifting sands; the jackal's tracks;*
> *The dirging wind; the wilderness of graves.*

The evening of September 13, the lofty Arch of Ctesiphon showed for hours as we toiled along the winding reaches; in the first gold and chill winds of dawn on the

14th we watched it recede. On the 18th I reached Beled, 'The Home of the Devil,' as the Arabs call it, where the Manchesters dragged out a panting existence, battling with dust-storms. In the station I was shocked to see what vandalism had been at work. The broken glass had been cleared away; in the tin shed where we had drunk tea amid the flying shrapnel on that Easter evening new panes had been put in; the water-tower had been replaced. With dusk I reached Samarra, and set Keely's mind at rest on the Greek girl question.

Through October Fritz came daily, photographing. The sole rays in a dreary protraction of existence were afforded by the Intelligence Summaries, run by Captain Lang, a versatile and popular humorist. Deserters reported that at a certain place the enemy's staff consisted of only one lame Turk and one 'powerful Christian.' The 'powerful Christian' had to do all the work, and was preparing for a hegira to our lines. Then we had exchanged prisoners recently, sending back eight wounded men, one having but one leg. On reaching the Turco lines, when we offered to give these wounded a further lift of some miles, the offer was accepted with cringing gratitude. 'Intelligence' surmised that these wounded might have to walk to Mosul, another hundred and forty miles, and went into reverie on the situation's possibilities. 'If the one-legged man has any influential friends in Constantinople, we may expect to hear shortly of a Turkish Commission in Iraq.' That was the time when the Report of the Mesopotamian Commission came out. Though a revelation in England, it did not excite us, who knew its facts long before. Then letters from the enemy G.H.Q. to General Maude had had his name and address printed on the envelope. This, 'Intelligence' thought, was sheer, outstanding swank, to show us that the Turks had at least one lithograph.

Late in September our second attempt on Ramadie met with complete success, when General Brooking captured the nucleus of a projected offensive against us. We by Tigris rejoiced, knowing, too, that our task, when it came, would be the easier.

The 1st Guides joined the division in place of the 'Bo-Peeps.' The brigades went out on reconnaissance frequently. September 25 saw one of these shows, which included a sham fight. The day was very hot, and Haigh's stretcher-bearers complained of the inconsiderate conduct of the thirty-one 'casualties.' 'Unfortunately there were no dead among them.' However, as one S.B. added, 'fortunately a good many died of wounds.' The 'died of wounds' were formed into platoons, and marched off the field of action.

The stretcher-bearer who made the remark about the 'died of wounds' was a particular friend of mine, who had a great gift of happy phrasing, illustrated in the words I have quoted. Once we had a long talk about the old battles, and, speaking of a common friend who had been killed, he observed, 'I do think it dreadful, his being killed like that—killed outright.' I never got at his notion of what made a cushy death; probably something Mexican or early mediaeval.

Through October my diary notes little but services and a terrible lecture on Mesopotamian history, which, from first to last, I delivered over fifty times. Latterly envious tongues alleged that I had to ask units for a parade when I gave this lecture. But those who said this lied saucily and shamelessly.

CHAPTER 6

# Huweslet; or, the Battle of Juber Island

*Night's blackness touched with red;*
*A cock's shrill clarion ringing;*
*Clamours for 'ruddy' buckets, Diamond's*[25] *bray;*
*Grousing of Johnson*[26] *tumbled out of bed;*
*And Fowke's falsetto, singing*
*'Is it nothing to you?'*
*So the battalion wakes, to march away*
*Heaven knows how far into the blue,*
*Heaven knows how many weary miles to do,*
*Till stars within some* nulla *watch us lie,*
*Worshipping sleep, while the icy hours drag by.*

October 22 was the date when Johnny developed unheard-of cheek. His patrols appeared by the river, one fellow riding along our wire and slashing it with his sword. Then from 1 p.m. onwards he shelled both banks of the river, having pushed down from his advanced post at Daur,

---

[25] The regimental (four-footed) donkey. The Leicestershires' hat badge is a black diamond.
[26] Needless to say, we had no 'Johnson.'

a dozen miles away, with a couple of hundred cavalry, several machine-guns, and light field-guns. The Guides and our cavalry were reported to have lost men and horses; and G.A., on picket, sent word that the Turks were digging themselves in. A and C Companies of the Leicestershires were out all day.

On the 23rd shelling continued, and that evening the division moved out. At the officers' meeting we were told that a force, estimated at four thousand Turks and several guns, was digging in. We were to do twelve thousand two hundred yards north, and then seven thousand five hundred yards half-right, to get behind them. This was the 28th Brigade. The 8th and 19th Brigades, starting later, were to make a frontal attack at 4 a.m.; our brigade were to enfilade the Turk when bolted; and these united efforts were to drive him into the dead ground by the river, and there, as the scheme wittily put it, our artillery and machine-guns would 'deal with him.' Whoever drew up the plan was not only bloody-minded but oblivious of long experience, assuming thus that John was such a very simple person.

We moved off just before dark, raising a white dust. Through all our wide detour there were strict injunctions against smoking, enforced among the Leicestershires, ignored among machine-gunners and Indian drivers. Never can night-march have been noisier. At every halt the mules sang down the whole length of the line; signallers and gunners clattered past. About midnight a stranger was seen talking to some *drabis*.[27] A Leicestershire sergeant, coming up, said, 'Hullo, it's a bloody Turk.' Hearing himself identified, Johnny turned round and saluted. He was led to the proper authorities, and proved to be a Turkish cadet. He was armed with a penknife and a pair of gloves.

---

[27] Indian drivers.

The night was bitterly cold. At 3.30 a.m. we 'rested.' We had reached what in Mesopotamia would be considered well-wooded country, an upland studded with bushes. Just on dawn we rose, with teeth chattering and limbs numbed with contact with the cold ground, and moved on. Our planes appeared, scouring the sky; and a few odd bursts of rifle-fire were heard about 7 a.m. We had now reached the edge of the dead ground against the river, and looked down to Tigris, as in later days I have looked down to the Jordan. The doctor and I were told to set up our aid-post in a deep *nulla* there, and wait on events. A report came from our air-folk that five thousand Turks were on Juber Island, opposite Huweslet.

We moved steadily forward to the attack, steadily but unbelievingly. Unbelief rose to positive derision, for as we topped a slight brow we gave a target no artillery could have resisted, yet nothing happened. 'It's a trap,' said Fowke darkly; 'he's luring us on.' Why should John lie doggo in this fashion? Nevertheless the airmen insisted that the Turks were there. So we dug ourselves in, in a semicircle facing the island, preliminary to attacking it. It was noon, hot and maddening with flies. The Leicestershires sent scouts out, who pushed up to Juber Island, and found that there were indeed five thousand there—five thousand sheep and several Arab shepherds.

On the opposite bank John had a machine-gun, with which he sniped those who approached the water. He killed mules, and wounded several *bhisties*[28] and a sweeper. There were also people sniping with rifles, and the Indian regiments had casualties. On our side, the cavalry brought in a prisoner. We had the young gentleman caught at night, and one other; the 19th Brigade took a fourth prisoner.

---

[28] Indian water-carriers.

So we abandoned the battle, had breakfast at 2.30 p.m., and returned. The day was wearying beyond conception, yet the men, British and Indian alike, were singing as they passed Al-Ajik. Samarra camp was a swirl of dust after the day's busyness; almost a fairy place in the last sunlight.

The next day was dedicated to sleep, and to humour at the expense of the Royal Flying Corps, to whose mess a sheep's head was voted.

## Chapter 7
# Daur

Johnny's leg-pull made him one up. This was recognized, and his action drew our attention to the undesirability of allowing him to remain at Daur. On October 31 the 28th Brigade went into the trenches at Al-Ajik. November 1 was Thursday. Haigh had the misfortune to go very sick on this day; he left us, and his successor arrived about 4 p.m. The new doctor fell into my hands, as the battalion was unknown to him, and he had never been in action.

As we went forward bad news came in, so bad and unexpected that it seemed incredible, the news of the Italian reverses. This filled us with profound depression. Our tiny side-show seemed more insignificant than ever while the European battle was being lost. When word followed of Allenby's success at Beersheba we did not guess that here was the beginning of a tide of victory which would ultimately pull the whole war our way. There was one splinter of light, an absurd joke in London Opinion which set the Leicestershires chuckling, 'Overheard at the Zoo.' It is the conversation of Cockney children before the ostrich cage:

'Sneagle!'
'Snotaneagle. Snork.'
'Snotanork. Snowl.'

'Snotanowl. Snostrich.'

This lent itself to indefinite expansion: 'Snemeu,' 'Snalbatross,' 'Snoriole,' 'Snelephant.'

Report came of the exploit of Marshall at Corps Head Quarters. He had gone out in a 'lamb'[29] on the other bank of Tigris, almost to Tekrit, and had shot down thirty horses and a dozen men as he flew past the enemy lines.

On the evening of November 1 the Al-Ajik trenches were crowded. Fritz came over reconnoitring, and his surprise was amusing to see. He checked, wheeled, abandoned all thought of a visit to our camp, and beetled back, after very elaborate reconnaissance. Then our own planes flew over, sounding their klaxons and dropping messages, in rehearsal for the morrow.

At 9.10 the force met at the place of assembly. The 21st Brigade were to move up the left bank; they are hardly in this picture. On the right bank the 28th Brigade went first, followed by the 19th and 8th Brigades. With the column were the 4th and 9th Brigades, R.F.A., two batteries of the 56th Brigade, and some 4.5 and 6-inch howitzers. Altogether, including those operating on the left bank, we had eighty guns.

The night was even colder than the one before the Juber Island farce. Part of the night I marched with my friends of the 53rd Sikhs, with Newitt and with Heathcote. Every one anticipated a very hard fight. We were up against a position which was reputed to be as strong as Istabulat had been. Before dawn we found ourselves among ghostly-looking bushes, and lay down for one shivering hour. We had marched over seventeen miles, with the usual exhausting checks and halts attendant on night-marching, and we were dead-beat to the wide. Yet nothing could

---

[29] Light-armoured motor-battery.

be finer than the way the men threw weariness away, like a garment, with the first shells, and went into battle.

Sarcka, the excellent Yank who ran our Y.M.C.A., marched with us, carrying a camel-load of cigarettes. He was usually called 'Carnegie' by Dr. Haigh. That classical mind memorized Sarcka's name as meaning 'flesh'; then, since it moved with equal ease in Greek and Latin, unconsciously transliterated. As we went forward, and a red sun rose over Tigris, Sarcka remarked: 'The sensation I am about to go through is one which I wouldn't miss for worlds.' Mester Dobson looked surprised. I bided my time, knowing how unpleasant the first fifteen minutes under shell-fire are for even the bravest.

Soon after 6 a.m. the enemy advanced pickets were driven in. We were advancing in artillery formation over undulating and broken country, sparsely set with *jujube*-bushes (*zizyphus*). A gazelle bounded away in front of us. At 6.15, says my diary, the first shells came. Our planes swept along, klaxons sounding, and the sky became torn with shrapnel. Johnny felt for us who formed the doctor's retinue, felt with an H.E. bracket, before and beyond us. The advance was extraordinarily rapid, a race; consequently the doctor's party got the benefit of most of this early shelling. Fortunately the enemy seemed to have got on to his old dumps, for his stuff, which came over plentifully enough, was detonating badly. A shell burst in Lyons's platoon, apparently under Lyons; yet he walked out of the dust unhurt. The 56th Rifles went first, advancing as if on parade; this day they rose high in the Leicestershires' admiration. The 'Tigers' came next; then the 51st and 53rd Sikhs. The enemy was fairly caught by surprise. Fritz, the previous day, had brought back the first hint that anything was doing; and, despite that knowledge, it was not expected that march and fight would come so swiftly and together. If the doctor stopped to bandage a man, we had to run to keep touch with the regiment. I was worried with visions of pockets of fifty or sixty wounded awaiting attention. Very early in the fight we found two men hit with shrapnel, and left them in the shell-hole. It was suggested to Sarcka that he stay with them, and guide the ambulances along our track whenever they came.

'No,' he said sturdily, 'I'm going on.'

And go on he did, and was shortly afterwards distributing cigarettes under heavy fire. Public opinion had condemned his coming, for the soldier holds that no man should go under fire unless he has a definite job there. But when he justified his place by a score of deeds, from cigarette-distributing to bandaging the wounded, public opinion rejoiced and accepted him, known for a comrade and a brave man.

Along the plain the enemy had a number of large thorn-stacks, with sand-bagged seats in their centres. Here had been snipers. These stacks we avoided; as we did, as a rule, all such things as battalion head quarters. The colonel of a regiment moves with a small army of orderlies; his majestic appearance over a brow rarely fails to draw a few salvoes. The doctor's meinie, therefore, took their way along the open, avoiding all prominences of landscape and people. I turned aside to what proved to be a 56th Rifles' aid-post, with a dead horse before it. Here had been the first Turkish lines. Our guns pushed on very rapidly, the gunners riding swiftly by and into a large, deep *nulla*. We over-passed them again; there was one smart minute or so when half a dozen 'pipsqueaks' burst in a narrow fault of the ground, scarcely a *nulla*, beside us, the steep sides killing the spread of the H.E. The enemy had been shrapnelling hard along the line occupied by the 56th Rifles and the Leicestershires. Nevertheless we picked up very few wounded.

Johnny's shrapnel now began to get wilder still. We found Colonel Brock, the Leicestershires' colonel, where several wide, big *nullas* met. The battalion was digging in, he said. About thirty prisoners came over a hill behind us. We set up an aid-post, our first stationary one; Sarcka produced a tin of Maconochie, and we had tiffin. A few wounded Indians came, the first being a man from whose pocket-book we extracted a shrapnel bullet. He had no other hurt.

The colonel was puzzled at our few casualties. There had been not only a good deal of shrapnel, but heavy rifle and machine-gun fire, yet hardly a man had been hit. The fight was nearly over, so I went back for ambulances. John was throwing a certain amount of explosive stuff about, uselessly and recklessly. On my way back I found Owen, of the 51st Sikhs, with a wounded arm. Owen, long ago, lost an eye in a bombing accident at Sannaiyat. He pluckily returned from India, and again took over the work of bombing instructor to his regiment.

It was now getting hot, being well past nine o'clock.

In the trenches by the 56th's aid-post there were two Turks, each with a leg smashed to pulp by H.E. But the most distressing sight was an enemy sniper on one of the O. Pips already mentioned. Round him were many used cartridges and bandoliers. He sat among the thorns, eight feet above ground, with the impassive mien of a Buddha. His face had been broken by our shrapnel, and his brains were running down it; the flies were busy on a clot of red brain by his temple. He was one mess of blood, and very heavy as well as high up. My efforts to lift him down simply stained my clothes.

About 4 p.m. I was with a doctor, looking at a dead Turk who was a particularly gruesome sight, with blood still dripping from his nose. Suddenly appeared a merchant with a camera, who took this Turk's photo. Not satisfied with this, he proceeded to stage-manage the place. The ambulance was coming up to remove a wounded Turk. He ordered it back, then bade it run up smartly, while the man was to be lifted in, equally smartly. Then he bade the doctor and myself stand behind the dead Turk aforementioned. When he went, the doctor said, 'Thank God, he's gone.' I took the man, in my carelessness, for another doctor with a taste for horrible pictures, and it was not till some time after that I realized he was the official cinematograph operator, and was merely doing his job. So, somewhere or other, a film has been exhibited, 'Wounded being collected on Mesopotamian battlefields.'

Going back to the Turkish sniper, who was still on his stack and had been overlooked by the cinematograph operator, I found that, in his agony, he had dug a hole in the thorns, and buried his head; I suppose, to escape the flies. His legs were waving feebly. It was right he should be left to the last, as he had no chance of life, and nothing could be done for him in any way. But never did I feel more the utter folly and silly cruelty of war than when I saw this brave man's misery. Next morning he was found to have crawled some hundreds of yards before dying. He had left his stack.

## Chapter 8
# Aujeh

Our line was where the plateau rose and then dropped steeply into deep, narrow fissures. The night was maddening with cold, and the rum ration came as a sheer necessity. All through this brief Tekrit campaign the British troops were without coats or blankets. The Indian troops had transport for theirs. The arrangement was correct in theory, since we came from a chill climate.

None of these later Mesopotamian pushes could be much more than raids. The rivers in this latitude were too shallow and shifting for transport, so we had to be fed and watered by means of Ford cars. It taxed the whole of the army's resources in Fords for Tekrit, blankets and coats having to give way to rations. Whilst the 7th Division pushed, the other two fronts were practically immobilized. Maude could strike on only one at a time of our three rivers. Ramadie was fought in September; Tekrit in November; Kifri in December; and the same round, of Euphrates, Tigris, and Diyaleh, was followed in 1918.

So we had ten days of what seemed arctic exposure. This night after Daur, Diggins shared a Burberry with me; nonetheless the night was one of insane wretchedness.

We rejoiced, with more than Vedic joy, to greet the dawn, though the flies swiftly made us long for night again.

On the 3rd we moved slightly forward. My brigade rested, while the 19th went on. The enemy's lines at Aujeh were taken easily. One wounded Turk was captured. He was set on a horse, and paraded restlessly back and forward, for some mystic reason, during the day. Fowke's solution was that the authorities hoped the troops would count him many times over, and been heartened by the thought that we had destroyed the Turks' last force in Mesopotamia. When the Aujeh lines had been taken, our cavalry, supported by the artillery, tried to rush Tekrit and burn the stores. This proved impracticable, so we shelled the dumps at long range. My brigade stood by, and watched from a high plateau the bursts and the great smoke-curtains which went up, as once from burning Sodom. The affair furnished Fowke with some excellent fooling. He would stand on a knoll and gnash his teeth, in Old Testament fashion declaiming, 'I will neither wash nor shave till Tekrit has fallen.' It is unnecessary to say that the vow was kept, and over kept; and not by Fowke alone. At other times he was plaintive and reproachful. We were shelling Tekrit—Tekrit, the Turkish base, where the Turkish hospitals were, and 'the pretty little Turkish nurses.' 'You chaps don't think about these things. You're selfish, and don't care. I do.'

The desultory fighting of this day was not without casualties. The 19th Brigade lost fifty-six men up to 2 p.m.; later I heard the figures were fourteen killed and seventy-three wounded. These were not in the 'taking' of the single line of Aujeh trenches, but came from long-distance shell-fire. The cavalry, too, lost men. The enemy slipped out on our coming, but their guns had the line beautifully registered. In the evening the 28th Brigade covered the cavalry's return. We had our own work as well. Fourteen shell-ammunition dumps fell into our hands by the enemy's retreat from Daur. These we collected, and quantities of shell-cases and wood. The Turkish gunners had most elaborate and comfortably-made dugouts, finely timbered. These were dismantled and fired. We marched in, with the hills ablaze about us, and the darkness warm and bright.

The 4th was Sunday. Fritz appeared about 6.30 a.m., and bombed us, coming very low indeed. Mesopotamia being a side-show for us, the enemy usually had at least one machine better than any of ours. This Sabbath Fritz spent in fetching bombs and distributing them. Twice he bombed the Leicestershires in the Turks' old trenches, but hit no one. So he paid no more attention to the infantry, but looked up the artillery, and the wagon-lines, and the transport. Here he did a deal of damage, and we soon had horses careering madly about the place. Reports came that the Turks were advancing. So, though no one dreamed that they would make a serious attack, we consolidated the last lines of the Daur position against them.

My diary notes: 'Rum ration. Flies.' For such elemental things had existence become memorable.

The day was cheered by news of the Gaza successes, as the previous day had been by that of Beersheba.

Fritz occupied his afternoon and evening in the same disreputable fashion. At nightfall our authorities were debating whether to go on to Tekrit or fall back to Samarra. Diggins, the fire-eater, hoped earnestly for the former course, and laid confident bets that it would be. Our brigadier, when I ran across him, deplored that in April we had stopped at Samarra, though he had urged our going on to Tekrit (or anywhere else where there were Turks).

Orders came. We were to fall back two miles, then sweep westward, and on to Tekrit. Fowke reiterated his engagement not to shave or wash till Tekrit had fallen; and we burned, with reluctant glee, the excellent wood that Johnny Turk had collected against our coming to Daur. Now in Mesopotamia wood is far, far more precious than rubies. But this wood had to be burned, since we were not coming back. So vast and glorious fires sprang up. And each hero, in his turn lifting a long beam, like a *phalarica*, hurled it at the blaze. The assembled Trojans cheered, with admiration or derision, according as each shot fell accurately or short. In this wise, then, did Sunday evening pass with the 17th Foot.

## Chapter 9
# Tekrit

We moved off, footsore. Mention of the cold must have become monotonous. But this night's cold touched a sharper nerve of agony than any before. Our 'rest' came, by a refinement of cruelty, not immediately before dawn, but between 2.30 and 4.30 a.m. We were then on bleak uplands, swept by arctic winds. In Baghdad winter is a time of frost; and we were far north of Baghdad. No men lay down; very few even stood still. The majority used the two hours of 'rest' in running to and fro, and it was with immense thankfulness that we took up our trudge once more.

This time there was no question of surprise. Morning found us on a vast plain, set with yellow-berried jujube-bushes and low scrub. Shortly after 6 a.m. the enemy began shelling our transport, which accordingly moved out of range. My brigade fell slightly back, in conformity. Captain McIntyre, in a gloomy mood perhaps due to the freezing night just finished, prophesied that we should get the 'heavy stuff' and the 'overs' when once the enemy gunners got their nefarious game fairly going. Everything was bustle. Signallers set up their posts, Head Quarters were established, caterpillars crawled up with their heavy guns. Lieutenant-General Cobbe, the First Corps commander, was controlling operations. Fritz also seemed interested. He came over twice, very low and very hurriedly, but did no bombing. His second visit was followed by half a dozen crumps, from the 5.9's, for our 6-inch guns.

This whole campaign had come very suddenly. Corps, I was told, were ignorant up to almost the day of our starting out from Samarra. Staff-captains and quartermasters received orders at the eleventh hour for transport arrangements. The campaign was a tour de force, everything being sacrificed to rations and water. A stream of Fords ran night and day between the troops and Samarra.

My brigade had a day of inaction, being moved up from time to time, and momentarily expecting to be sent in. The 21st Brigade had moved up the left bank, meeting with no opposition. Their part was enfilade gunfire. Our old colleagues, the 8th Brigade (from the 3rd Lahore Division), and the 19th Brigade attacked. The battle was largely one of gunfire. For such an exhibition Guy Fawkes' Day had been fitly chosen.

Tekrit was one of the Turk's best battles in the class of which he is such a master, the rearguard action. Our airmen reported that, from our arrival, his troops and transport were flowing away steadily. His lines were held by artillery and machine-guns, fearlessly worked to the last minute of safety. Our cavalry operated on the left. It was here the action broke down. At this point there was only one line of trenches against us, and many think the 28th Brigade should have been sent in. Had this been done, the enemy right would have been forced back, and his troops pinned to the river, with large captures of men and guns as result. But the 28th Brigade were kept out, because of a cavalry mistake. The latter's orders were to drop one brigade on the flank, and then push through to the river, behind the enemy. Then the 28th Brigade were to go in, and, when they had cleared the Turks out of their entrenchments, the cavalry were to collect the prisoners. But, instead, the cavalry, after dropping a brigade to watch the flank, waited, and finally did a very gallant but useless charge.

The terrain was extremely difficult. Almost the first thing the assaulting forces had to do was to cross a *nulla* sixty feet deep and a quarter of a mile wide, commanded by machine-guns, and searched with shrapnel. Later, when my own brigade moved up in support, we crossed this *nulla*. The toilsome going over slipping shingle was like Satan's painful steps on the burning marl,

> *not like those steps*
> *On Heaven's azure, and the torrid clime*
> *Smote on him sore besides, vaulted with fire.*

The story of this day belongs to the 8th and 19th Brigades. My own were spectators only; deeply interested, and our own fate might at any moment become involved, but harassed with heat and flies and the unspeakable boredom born of long warfare, which even a battle can disperse only in part. Stories filtered through of the heroic work of the Seaforths and Manchesters and of the 47th and 59th Sikhs. Report persisted that the Seaforths' head quarters had been knocked out by a direct hit, with twelve casualties, and that their regimental sergeant-major (Sutherland) was killed. This rumour was partly true, but a little exaggerated. Their colonel (Reginald Schomberg) was wounded, and their adjutant (McRae). This was the McRae who had fought the Turks with his naked fists at Sheikh Saad in January, 1916, and who rose from sergeant-major to Lieutenant-Colonel, with D.S.O. and Bar. Sutherland was not killed, but wounded. Lee, the Seaforths' padre, kept up the tradition set by Dr. Ewing, that 'unsubduable old Roman' whose white locks had waved through so many battles, till he was wounded at the forcing of Baghdad. Burn, the one Seaforths' officer killed, out of twelve hit, was struck close behind Lee. Milne and Baldry were killed among the Manchesters' officers.

From 10.30 to 11 a.m. was a time of artillery preparation. Fritz drifted restlessly about; our own planes were busy; klaxons sounded; messages were dropped. According to information, opposite us the Turkish 51st and 52nd Divisions were unsupported. Both were old foes of Sannaiyat days. By 11.30 the enemy's first two lines were taken by direct assault. At 3 p.m. my own brigade moved two miles closer in, on the left. It was a costly business, pushing the enemy back by frontal attack just where he was strongest in every way. Long lines of our wounded passed us, with a few Turkish prisoners. The day was as intolerably hot as the night had been cold. By four o'clock the Turk had got most of his heavier guns back. We were shelling a small mosque, which he was using as an O.P. The 6-inches registered a hit, which sent up a white cloud of dust and powder. Every one was hopeful. The cavalry and 'lambs' were said to be right round the enemy's flank, and some thousands of prisoners were regarded as certain. Captain Henderson, the Diggins of the Manchesters, was rumoured to have taken three guns. At 4.30 the 21st Brigade launched an effective enfilade on the enemy's transport from across the river; the two attacking brigades went in again; the cavalry charged across the Turks' right trenches. We of the 28th could watch it all with the naked eye, the one confusion being sometimes as to whether it was Turks scurrying away or Seaforths going in. But we saw the Seaforths' magnificent charge. Unfortunately most of the crumps which we took to be among a Turkish counter-attack were among our own men, who at one time ran into their own barrage. Their line swept forward, irresistible as always. In later days, in Palestine, when a despatch praised various miscellaneous troops who had been in their first actions and done not too badly, some one was foolish enough to express surprise that the Seaforths were not mentioned by name. 'I should consider it an insult,' said their colonel, 'if any one thought it worth mentioning that my regiment had done what they were told to do. We take some things for granted.' At Tekrit Schomberg, though already wounded, led his men in person. He was scholar and Christian; 'the bravest of the brave,' yet a lover of all fair things.

As the Turks ran from their trenches our machine-guns cut them up. Rumour now grew positive that we had the enemy hemmed against the river. Evening closed with a deal of desultory gunfire, which continued spasmodically all night. My brigade went to rest, in anticipation of a renewal of battle next dawn, when our turn would be due. The ambulances had worked nobly all day, cars sweeping up to well within shell-range; and all night long stretcher-bearer parties were busy. Their work was superintended by Captain Godson, whose M.C. was well earned.

Tekrit cost us about two thousand casualties. Many of the wounded collected in the 19 C.C.S.[30] at Samarra had been wounded by aeroplane bombs.

Next morning our orders of the previous night were confirmed. The enemy were supposed to be holding the 'kilns' (actually these were tombs) behind Tekrit. The 28th Brigade were to go through the 8th and 19th Brigades, and drive them out. We were very doubtful of

---

[30] Casualty clearing-station.

their being there. However, we went forward in the usual artillery formation. Every house in Tekrit had a white flag. This was the place where Townshend's men were spat on as they limped through it, prisoners. Nevertheless there was the same surprising display of fairly clean linen to which the villages before Baghdad had treated us eight months previously, and the Arabs were most anxious for us to realize how extremely friendly their sentiments were.

We went forward, but found the Turks had gone. There were crump-holes everywhere; the amount of our shrapnel lying about, wasted, would have broken a Chancellor of the Exchequer's heart. Parts of the spaces between the Turkish successive lines were just contiguous craters. But there had been disappointingly few direct hits on trenches. The cemetery, hard by, possessed one or two craters also. The enemy had left abundant live shells, shell-cases, cartridge-cases. But there were very few dead. I saw only two; and a few places where the parapet had been pulled in for a hasty burial. The old question was raised, Did the Turk dig graves beforehand, against an action, to hide his losses? If he did, one can imagine few more effective ways of putting heart into his troops than by detailing them for such a job. I heard that the Seaforths buried sixty Turks. But their losses were certainly far less than ours. We took a hundred and fifty-seven prisoners. Corps claimed that evidence collected after the battle showed that the enemy losses for the three actions of Daur, Aujeh, Tekrit, were at least fifteen hundred. The Infantry, who had not access to Corps' means of information, assessed them much lower. Myself, I think eight hundred would be nearer the mark.

There were great heaps of cartridge-cases, at intervals

of fifty yards, along the trenches, where machine-gunners had clearly been. The spaces between showed little sign of having been held. From the Turk's point of view, Tekrit was as satisfactory a battle almost as, from our point of view, it was unsatisfactory. His gunners and machine-gunners fought with very great skill and coolness, withdrawing late and rapidly; hence the great dumps of shell-ammunition which were our only booty. We should have got the whole force. But no sufficient barrage was kept up on the lines of retreat during the night; the cavalry's service, though gallant, was ineffective; the 28th Brigade were not used at the one point where they might have done the enemy much harm; and Head Quarters were too far back. The Turks got every gun and machine-gun away. We captured a hundred boxes of field-gun ammunition, four hundred rifles, five thousand wooden beams, gun-limbers, boats, bridging material, buoys, two aeroplanes (one utterly broken up by the enemy, the other repairable), and a box of propellers, all serviceable. The enemy blew up three ammunition dumps before retreating.

Fowke had dragged through the campaign with a crocked knee. He now went into hospital. There J.Y., who always anxiously haunted all battle-purlieus, fearing for the regiment he loved so well, found him; and, since he was not ill, obtained permission to feed him with some of the battalion's Christmas pudding, just arrived. He refreshed him, too, with Kirin beer. Thus J.Y.'s last glimpse of him—for Fowke did not return to the battalion—was a happy one.

These days were very wretched. Turkish camps are unbelievably filthy; and flies swarmed on the battlefield. We salvaged some miles up beyond Tekrit, with the results already stated. One of the two captured planes was a recovered one of our own, with the enemy black painted over our sign. We had a lot of very enjoyable destruction, including that of the musketry school and barracks, four miles away.

Tekrit's chief fame is that Saladin was born just outside it. But it was also an early Christian centre; the town wall is said to be partly the old monastery wall. The town is built on cliffs, which tower very steeply above the Tigris. The inhabitants were keen on trade, taking anything 'not too hot or too heavy'; but were unpleasant and exorbitant beyond any Arabs, even of Mesopotamia.

We now held both the Tigris and the Euphrates ends of the caravan route to Hit. G.A. opined that we should drive the enemy in from both ends, till both British forces were shelling each other. However, the Turk ran some seventy miles farther; and our planes did great bombing raids on their camp in the Jebel Hamrin, having the joy of using some of the enemy's own bombs.

On the 8th I got a lift back to Samarra on a Ford, for the purpose of sending up food and comforts to the battalion. This kindly purpose was never fulfilled. I went sick, but had more sense than to go to hospital this time; and the troops returned from Tekrit. The Leicestershires on route put up a large hyena, but failed to run him down. My premature return became a famous taunt. 'He deserted,' Diggins would say when foiled in fair argument; 'deserted from Tekrit, deserted in face of the enemy.'

The troops were back at Samarra by the 13th. 'Ah!' Busra surmised, 'they've had a bad knock. "Withdrawn on account of difficulty of communications." We know that story.' It was as after the April fighting, when the wildest distortions were believed down the line, and when I was asked in confidence by an officer formerly with the

Leicestershires if it was true that his old regiment had lost eighteen of our own guns.

Nearly every one was seedy for a while, with chills on the stomach and sore feet; and a great wave of depression passed over the division. We would have made any effort to hold Tekrit after our toil and losses. But the Fords were needed for another front. So Johnny, after a time, was able to creep cautiously back, to the extent of cavalry patrols at Daur and Tekrit.

CHAPTER 10

# Down to Busra

Events moved rapidly for the division. The brigades scattered down the line, and H.Q. went to Akab, near the supposed site of Opis. The 21st Brigade went across the river. Only the Leicestershires remained at Samarra, and even they sent one company to Istabulat. Our other three companies went to the station. The 3rd Division took over Istabulat and Samarra. The conviction took root that we were leaving the country.

On the 19th General Maude's death was told. A pack of rumours came as to how he had come to die, and as to how many others had died. His funeral took place in Baghdad; Fritz attended and dropped a message of sympathy. Mistaking his purpose when he flew so low, the archies fired on him. Also, for once, they are said to have nearly hit him.

Knowledge of the magnitude of the Italian reverses filtered in. Our Baghdad Anzac wireless heard 'one hundred thousand prisoners,' when the German wireless broke in, 'Hallo, hallo, hallo, Baghdad! We can tell you later news. It is three hundred thousand prisoners, two thousand five hundred guns.' The enemy wireless possessed the code-name of our own, and frequently broke in on our messages with information, asking us to acknowledge; but this was forbidden.

In December's first week the Kifri push took place. This was not the 7th Division's affair. The Third Corps had it in charge. We rationed them, which meant thirty-five miles of communications, up the left bank of the Tigris, into the sub-hills of the Persian borderlands. The 20th Punjabis furnished dump-guards. These days I spent, exceedingly pleasantly, with the Guides in the Adhaim Valley. Here was a scene of exquisite loveliness. The Adhaim was dry; but, in its deep bed, green lines showed where the water ran. The winter floods were even then beginning to gather higher up, and had reached to within a dozen miles of the brook's junction with Tigris. The valley was thick jungle. There were no trees, but a most dense and luxuriant growth of tamarisk, *populus euphratica*, *zizyphs* and other thorns, forming a covert six to fourteen feet high. Liquorice grew freely. Wild pig abounded, hares, black partridge, and *sisi*. In my very brief stay I saw no pig; but their signs were everywhere, and their water-holes in the river-bed bore marks of constant resort. The Adhaim was crossed by Nebuchadnezzar's great Nahrwan Canal. This was now, in effect, a deep *nulla*, and had silted in, so that its bottom was above the Adhaim bank. Its cliffs were tenanted with blue rock-pigeon, with hedgehogs and porcupines. Shoals of mackerel-like fish used to swim up the Tigris, with fins skimming the surface. Erskine showed me how to shoot these; as, in later days, when we were in the Palestine line at Arsuf, I have seen Diggins stunning fish with rifle-shots in the old Roman harbour.

In their Samarra digging the Guides had found a stone statue, which is what they asked me up to see. The head and arms had been broken off, obviously deliberately; but it was plainly the Goddess Ishtar, with breasts remaining. She was sitting before the mess-tent, like Demeter before the House of Triptolemus. This discovery was of interest beyond itself. The books place Opis near Akab, apparently because the Adhaim enters the Tigris opposite Akab. But, as I have said already, Kenneth Mason has accumulated good reasons for placing Opis near Samarra. With those reasons, this statue of Ishtar may take its place. The Samarra of history was not much more than a standing camp for caliphs in refuge from their true capital, Baghdad. But old Samarra covers nearly twenty square miles of ruins upon ruins. Opis was a great mart; and Samarra, in the relics of Eski Baghdad, to the north, reaches almost to the Tigris end of the Tekrit-Hit caravan road.

The Kifri push resulted in another withdrawal of the fight-weary John. He set Kifri coal-mine on fire, and it burned for some days. We took a hundred and fifty prisoners and two field-guns. Though Russia was out of the war, a local force of Russians helped us. They were told they would find their rations in a certain place when they took it. They took it all right.

I left the Guides, and went back to Beled, to my good friends of the 56th Brigade, R.F.A. On December 6 the 19th Infantry and the 56th Artillery Brigades received orders to move down-stream immediately. All came suddenly; I was awakened by the striking of tents. On the 8th the Leicestershires left Samarra. In less than six days they were in Baghdad. In those six days of marching they suffered terribly from cold, rain, and footsoreness. But they swung through Baghdad singing. The men of the Anzac wireless bought up oranges, and threw them to our fellows as they passed out of Baghdad to their camp at Hinaidi, two miles below. Baghdad streets were frozen every morning; a bucket of water, put out overnight, would be almost solid next day. Nevertheless there were enough flies to be an intolerable pest. When we passed the variously spelt station of Mushaidiyeh, Keely noted the script preferred by the railway, Mouchâhadie, and observed, 'Evidently it was connected in their mind with flies; no doubt with good reason.'

Baghdad in winter is given up to immense flocks of crows and starlings and to the 'Baghdad canary.'[31] No wild flowers were out, except a white *alisma*. We purchased 'goodly Babylonish garments,' the *abbas* for which the town is famous. Mine were sent home in an oil-sheet. The oil-sheet arrived, the postal-service satisfying themselves with looting the *abbas*. After all, men who have the monotony of service at the Base are entitled to indemnify themselves for the trouble to which men up the line put them.

We got our last glimpse of Fritz on the 15th. He was over Baghdad, and was said to have dropped a message, 'Good-bye, 7th Division.' The countryside was stiff with troops moving up and down.

Our destination was matter of constant speculation. When orders to leave Beled reached the 19th Brigade, there came a wire from Divisional Head Quarters, 'Tell the padre to preach from Matthew twenty, verse eighteen.' But the 28th Brigade knew nothing of this hint to Lee. Some thought we were going to Ahwaz, and thence up to Persia; others held this Persian theory with a modification, that we should arrive up-country from Bushire. The favourite notion was that we were going to do another Gallipoli landing, behind Alexandretta. Some one got hold of a map, and announced that there were mountains there nine thousand feet high.

---

[31] The domestic ass.

On the 18th we embarked, and began our slow drift down the flooded, racing stream. We passed the old landmarks, so known and so remembered. On the 20th we passed Kut, and knew that for most of us it was our farewell glimpse of the town that through so many dreadful months had seemed a place of fairy, and inaccessible.

*Red Autumn on the banks,*
*Where, through fields that bear no grain,*
*A desolate Mother treads,*
*By the brimming river, torn with rain!*
*A chill wind moves in the faded ranks*
*Of the rushes, rumpling their russet heads.*
*And out of the mist, on the racing stream*
*As I drift, I know that there gathers fast,*
*Over the lands I shall see no more,*
*Another mist, which with life shall last,*
*Till all that I watched and my comrades bore*
*Will be autumn mist, in an old man's dream.*

Here an Empire's might had agonized; and many of us had buried more hopes than we shall cherish again.

It rained, and kept on raining. Knowing what wretchedness this meant on shore, we were glad of the crowded shelter of our P-boat, maugre its noises and discomforts. Marshall, the semi-mythical person at Corps, who had visited the Turks at Tekrit, scattering ruin from a 'lamb,' was everywhere said to be taking bets, ten to one, that the war would be ended by Christmas. If rumour spoke truth, Marshall must have lost a pile of money.

On the 22nd we entrained at Amara, reaching Busra late on the 23rd. We spent Christmas encamped on a marsh. My mare developed unsuspected gifts as a humorist. Every time she saw a tree, even a date-palm, she shied, cavorted, and leapt, showing the utmost amazement and terror. This was witty at first, but she kept it up too long. Busra backwaters were lovelier than ever, with the willows in their winter dress, gold-streaked, and the brooding blue kingfishers above the waveless channels. Bablas[32] were in yellow button, scenting the ditches where huge tortoises crawled and clustered. On the 30th I got a glimpse of Shaiba, of the tall feathery tamarisks above the Norfolks' graves and trenches. On January 2 we embarked on the Bandra. With the cheering as we moved away, the words of a Mesopotamian 'gaff'[33] recurred to memory:

*And when we came to Ashar,[34] we only cheered once;*
*And I don't suppose we shall cheer again,*
   *for months, and months, and months.*

We drifted down the beautiful waterway, past its forest of palms and its abundant willows and waving reeds. We reached Koweit Bay on the 4th and waited for rations and our new boats. On the 7th we were on our way to a new campaign. In nine months the Leicestershires were swinging through Beirut in the old, immemorial fashion, though foot-weary, and singing, whilst the people madly cheered and shouted. But it was not the old crowd. Fowke, Warren, Burrows—these three were gathered, two months after the battalion left Mesopotamia, at Kantara, when the German last offensive burst. They were sent at once to France. Fowke and Warren were badly wounded; a letter from Fowke informed me that he was hit 'while running away,' a jesting statement which one understands. Burrows, one of our keenest minds and a delightful man, a valued friend, did extraordinarily well—he was strangely fearless—but was killed

---

[32] Mimosa.
[33] Concert party.
[34] At Busra; the place of disembarkation.

as the French war was ending. From the 19th Brigade Haughton, Thornhill, General Peebles, had all gone long ago. Haughton was wounded in the Afghan War, and Thornhill died of illness. And now, as I write, G.A. is off to South America again, and J.Y. to Canada.

*I and my friends have seen our friends no more.*

# ALSO FROM LEONAUR
### AVAILABLE IN SOFTCOVER OR HARDCOVER WITH DUST JACKET

**SEPOYS, SIEGE & STORM** by Charles John Griffiths—The Experiences of a young officer of H.M.'s 61st Regiment at Ferozepore, Delhi ridge and at the fall of Delhi during the Indian mutiny 1857.

**CAMPAIGNING IN ZULULAND** by W. E. Montague—Experiences on campaign during the Zulu war of 1879 with the 94th Regiment.

**THE STORY OF THE GUIDES** by G. J. Younghusband—The Exploits of the Soldiers of the famous Indian Army Regiment from the northwest frontier 1847 - 1900..

**ZULU: 1879** by D.C.F. Moodie & the Leonaur Editors—The Anglo-Zulu War of 1879 from contemporary sources: First Hand Accounts, Interviews, Dispatches, Official Documents & Newspaper Reports.

**THE RECOLLECTIONS OF SKINNER OF SKINNER'S HORSE** by James Skinner—James Skinner and his 'Yellow Boys' Irregular cavalry in the wars of India between the British, Mahratta, Rajput, Mogul, Sikh & Pindarree Forces.

**TOMMY ATKINS' WAR STORIES 14 FIRST HAND ACCOUNTS**—Fourteen first hand accounts from the ranks of the British Army during Queen Victoria's Empire Original & True Battle Stories Recollections of the Indian Mutiny With the 49th in the Crimea With the Guards in Egypt The Charge of the Six Hundred With Wolseley in Ashanti Alma, Inkermann and Magdala With the Gunners at Tel-el-Kebir Russian Guns and Indian Rebels Rough Work in the Crimea In the Maori Rising Facing the Zulus From Sebastopol to Lucknow Sent to Save Gordon On the March to Chitral Tommy by Rudyard Kipling

**CHASSEUR OF 1914** by Marcel Dupont—Experiences of the twilight of the French Light Cavalry by a young officer during the early battles of the great war in Europe.

**TROOP HORSE & TRENCH** by R. A. Lloyd—The experiences of a British Lifeguardsman of the household cavalry fighting on the western front during the First World War 1914-18.

**THE EAST AFRICAN MOUNTED RIFLES** by C. J. Wilson—Experiences of the campaign in the East African bush during the First World War.

**THE FIGHTING CAMELIERS** by Frank Reid—The exploits of the Imperial Camel Corps in the desert and Palestine campaigns of the First World War.

### AVAILABLE ONLINE AT
## www.leonaur.com
### AND OTHER GOOD BOOK STORES

# ALSO FROM LEONAUR
### AVAILABLE IN SOFTCOVER OR HARDCOVER WITH DUST JACKET

**THE COMPLEAT RIFLEMAN HARRIS** by *Benjamin Harris as told to & transcribed by Captain Henry Curling*—The adventures of a soldier of the 95th (Rifles) during the Peninsular Campaign of the Napoleonic Wars

**WITH WELLINGTON'S LIGHT CAVALRY** by *William Tomkinson*—The Experiences of an officer of the 16th Light Dragoons in the Peninsular and Waterloo campaigns of the Napoleonic Wars.

**SERGEANT BOURGOGNE** by *Adrien Bourgogne*—With Napoleon's Imperial Guard in the Russian Campaign and on the Retreat from Moscow 1812 - 13.

**SWORDS OF HONOUR** by *Henry Newbolt & Stanley L. Wood*—The Careers of Six Outstanding Officers from the Napoleonic Wars, the Wars for India and the American Civil War, with dozens of illustrations by Stanley L. Wood.

**SURTEES OF THE RIFLES** by *William Surtees*—A Soldier of the 95th (Rifles) in the Peninsular campaign of the Napoleonic Wars.

**ENSIGN BELL IN THE PENINSULAR WAR** by *George Bell*—The Experiences of a young British Soldier of the 34th Regiment 'The Cumberland Gentlemen' in the Napoleonic wars.

**HUSSAR IN WINTER** by *Alexander Gordon*—A British Cavalry Officer during the retreat to Corunna in the Peninsular campaign of the Napoleonic Wars.

**NAPOLEONIC WAR STORIES** by *Sir Arthur Quiller-Couch*—Tales of soldiers, spies, battles & sieges from the Peninsular & Waterloo campaingns.

**JOURNALS OF ROBERT ROGERS OF THE RANGERS** by *Robert Rogers*—The exploits of Rogers & the Rangers in his own words during 1755-1761 in the French & Indian War.

**KERSHAW'S BRIGADE VOLUME 1** by *D. Augustus Dickert*—Manassas, Seven Pines, Sharpsburg (Antietam), Fredricksburg, Chancellorsville, Gettysburg, Chickamauga, Chattanooga, Fort Sanders & Bean Station..

**KERSHAW'S BRIGADE VOLUME 2** by *D. Augustus Dickert*—At the wilderness, Cold Harbour, Petersburg, The Shenandoah Valley and Cedar Creek.

**A TIGER ON HORSEBACK** by *L. March Phillips*—The Experiences of a Trooper & Officer of Rimington's Guides - The Tigers - during the Anglo-Boer war 1899 - 1902.

### AVAILABLE ONLINE AT
## www.leonaur.com
### AND OTHER GOOD BOOK STORES

## ALSO FROM LEONAUR
### AVAILABLE IN SOFTCOVER OR HARDCOVER WITH DUST JACKET

**CAPTAIN OF THE 95th (Rifles)** *by Jonathan Leach*—An officer of Wellington's Sharpshooters during the Peninsular, South of France and Waterloo Campaigns of the Napoleonic Wars.

**THE KHAKEE RESSALAH** *by Robert Henry Wallace Dunlop*—Service & adventure with the Meerut volunteer horse during the Indian mutiny 1857-1858

**BUGLER AND OFFICER OF THE RIFLES** *by William Green & Harry Smith* With the 95th (Rifles) during the Peninsular & Waterloo Campaigns of the Napoleonic Wars

**BAYONETS, BUGLES AND BONNETS** *by James 'Thomas' Todd*—Experiences of hard soldiering with the 71st Foot - the Highland Light Infantry - through many battles of the Napoleonic wars including the Peninsular & Waterloo Campaigns

**A NORFOLK SOLDIER IN THE FIRST SIKH WAR** *by J W Baldwin*—Experiences of a private of H.M. 9th Regiment of Foot in the battles for the Punjab, India 1845-46

**A CAVALRY OFFICER DURING THE SEPOY REVOLT** *by A.R.D. Mackenzie*—Experiences with the 3rd Bengal Light Cavalry, the Guides and Sikh Irregular Cavalry from the outbreak to Delhi and Lucknow

**THE ADVENTURES OF A LIGHT DRAGOON** *by George Farmer & G.R. Gleig*—A cavalryman during the Peninsular & Waterloo Campaigns, in captivity & at the siege of Bhurtpore, India

**THE COMPLEAT RIFLEMAN HARRIS** *by Benjamin Harris as told to & transcribed by Captain Henry Curling*—The adventures of a soldier of the 95th (Rifles) during the Peninsular Campaign of the Napoleonic Wars

**THE RED DRAGOON** *by W.J. Adams*—With the 7th Dragoon Guards in the Cape of Good Hope against the Boers & the Kaffir tribes during the 'war of the axe' 1843-48

**THE LIFE OF THE REAL BRIGADIER GERARD - Volume 1 - THE YOUNG HUSSAR 1782 - 1807** *by Jean-Baptiste De Marbot*—A French Cavalryman Of the Napoleonic Wars at Marengo, Austerlitz, Jena, Eylau & Friedland

**THE LIFE OF THE REAL BRIGADIER GERARD Volume 2 IMPERIAL AIDE-DE-CAMP 1807 - 1811** *by Jean-Baptiste De Marbot*—A French Cavalryman of the Napoleonic Wars at Saragossa, Landshut, Eckmuhl, Ratisbon, Aspern-Essling, Wagram, Busaco & Torres Vedras

### AVAILABLE ONLINE AT
### www.leonaur.com
### AND OTHER GOOD BOOK STORES

www.ingramcontent.com/pod-product-compliance
Lightning Source LLC
Chambersburg PA
CBHW021009090426
42738CB00007B/716